Pilot
in *The Danish Brigade*
in Sweden
during the Second World War

Aage Sandqvist

BoD

© 2021 Sandqvist, Aage
Publisher: BoD – Books on Demand, Stockholm, Sweden
Printer: BoD – Books on Demand, Norderstedt, Germany
ISBN: 978-91-7969-219-3

Contents

PART 1: Denmark, 1930 - 1944

PART 2: Sweden, 1944 - 1945

Preface

I was born in Denmark on June 1, 1939, and my childhood was somewhat unusual, partly because of the prevailing war situation, and partly because I lived on Aalborg Airport after the war until I was 12 years old. In 1951 my family emigrated to Canada, and I became a Canadian citizen when I turned 18. My studies took me to the University of Maryland, USA, where I obtained a doctorate in astronomy. Here I also met my wife, who was then a Swedish exchange student. In 1971 we moved to Sweden, where we later had three children, and I eventually became a Swedish citizen. My career as an astronomer culminated in my becoming a professor of astronomy at Stockholm University, where I am now a professor emeritus.

Throughout my childhood and as long as my father lived, I have heard exciting stories about his life as a pilot in Denmark before the Second World War, and his experience as a resistance adversary during the war – how he was captured by the Germans, put in concentration camps, and fled by jumping off a moving military transport train, where he had been placed as a hostage. During a couple of visits to my parents in Canada in the early 1980s, I recorded my father as he related his stories. These tapes, as well as his photo and newspaper-clipping albums, are partly the basis for Part 1 of this book.

However, my father never told me about what happened after he and his wife escaped to Sweden, while my brother and I remained in Denmark with relatives and friends. I suspect that my father's silence was due to his great respect for state secrets, and Sweden's departure from neutrality when giving aid to Denmark and Danish refugees during the second half of the war. Handing over some of its best aircraft to a few Danish pilots in the Danish Brigade in Sweden must surely be considered counter to Sweden's stated neutrality. To investigate what happened to my father in Sweden, I have spent many hours in the Swedish War Archives and the Swedish National Archives, where I have found new documents, some of which retained their secrecy status until 2011. Also, I was again greatly aided by my father's photo and newspaper-clipping albums. The Swedish episode constitutes Part 2 of this book.

My father, Lieutenant Carlo Hjalmar Sandqvist, is the "Pilot in the Danish Brigade in Sweden during the Second World War".

Aage Sandqvist,
Saltsjöbaden, Sweden, in June, 2021

Acknowledgements

First of all, I thank my wife, **Karin Sandqvist**, for her enduring patience with all my questions regarding the language, grammar and spelling in the original Swedish version of this book, as well as for her many comments on the manuscript.

Next, a large dose of gratitude is due to my "supervisor" in this project, Captain Dr. **Roland Karlsson**, who, with his extensive experience and personal network in the Swedish aviation world, has opened many doors in my handling of Part 2 of this book. He, together with his wife, **Marianne Sahlin-Karlsson**, head of Quality Safety & Security Management at the Swedish Civil Aviation Administration, has read the entire Swedish and English manuscripts and made many suggestions for improvements.

A real goldmine to Danish aviation history, not least in the case of the Danish Brigade's Air Unit, is Captain **Niels Helmø Larsen.** To him, I should like to express my great appreciation for supplying historical anecdotes and photos, and also for acting as my host at Værløse Airport during a major air show day in 2017.

I have also received great help with photos from **Ove Larsson**, Museum Manager at F7 Gårds & Flottiljmuseum, who also hosted me during a visit to F7 Såtenäs Air Base in 2016.

A particular mention goes to **Anders Chr. Johansen**, who in 2001 showed me around my old childhood home, Aalborg Airport, the military as well as the civilian part.

A big thank you is due to **Michael Sanz**, Office Manager at the Swedish Aviation Historical Society's office in Stockholm,

For help with photos and other material, I should like to thank **Jan Forsgren** Arlanda Flygsamlingar, **Torben Jørgensen** Danish Aviation Historical Society, **Per Kustvik** Saab, **Jens Langeland-Knudsen** Denmark, **Henrik Lundbak** Museum of Danish Resistance, **Jenny Melin** Mønthuset Denmark, **Lisa Gyde Nielsen** Aalborg Airport, **Ditte Trudslev** and **Henrik Abildgaard Christensen** Aalborg City Archive.

My children, **Tor**, **Inga**, and **Leif,** have contributed helpful comments. I have received excellent help with the Danish language from **Ulla Sparrevohn,** and my brother **Erik** who also took the photo on the last page of the book.

Prologue: Såtenäs, Sweden, May 4 - 5, 1945

Saturday, May 5, 1945.

Early Saturday morning, eight of Sweden's best bomber aircraft, Saab B17, stood with their propellers spinning at the F7 Air Base in Såtenäs. It lies on the shore of Lake Vänern in mid-Sweden. In front of the aeroplanes, eight Danish pilots, with technicians and mechanics, were busy preparing for lift-off and heading towards Denmark. All the Swedish aircraft had been painted with Danish nationality designations – clearly violating Sweden's declared neutrality. In essence, the Danish Army Air Troops designations had been painted on both the upper and lower sides of the wings, and the Danish naval flag was painted on the stabilizer. Only one part was missing, namely the order "to start". So, the warming of the engines carried on, and on, and on ...

In the morning of the day before, these Danish pilots and technicians had arrived at F7 Såtenäs from two other airbases in Sweden, F6 Karlsborg and F12 Kalmar. During many months, they had been training to be ready for deployment as support for the Danish Brigade's relief efforts to end the German occupation of Denmark, which were expected to take place near the end of World War II. (The third group of Danish pilots and technicians from F4 Östersund would arrive at F7 Såtenäs on May 6).

One of the Danish pilots from F6 Karlsborg was Lieutenant Carlo Hjalmar Sandqvist. He had prepared a plan for a B17 attack on the Danish airport in Aalborg, with which he was well acquainted from both before and during the war. This airport was the most important springboard to Norway for the Germans, and also functioned as a base for German air patrols over the northern part of the North Sea. The attack plan had just been presented to the groups at F7 Såtenäs.

In the evening of May 4, Carlo and a friend had been strolling in the pleasant park behind the magnificent manor building, which now housed the officers' mess. When he returned to the officers' mess, it was empty, which puzzled him. The two friends sat down to listen to the radio. They were surprised to hear national and patriotic tunes. It was evident that something important had happened. Finally, they discovered that the other Danish pilots were at the home of the F7 airbase commander, Lieutenant Colonel Folke Ramström. He had invited them to a dinner to celebrate a dramatic message, which had just arrived from Field Marshal Montgomery's headquarters in Northern Germany: "The German troops in Holland, Denmark and Northwestern Germany have surrendered."

The "Danish" Saab B17C:s at F7 Såtenäs, May 5, 1945
(Photo : F7 Museum)

PART 1: Denmark, 1930 - 1944

Chapter 1: International Aviation Meeting Zürich, July 22 - 31, 1932

Wednesday, July 20, 1932.

The 22-year-old Carlo sat in his two-winged Fokker C. V-E, behind the humming Bristol Jupiter engine. Carlo was on his way to the adventure of his life. It was only one year since he had been selected among over 400 applicants as one of seven admitted to Hærens Flyveskole (the Army's Flying School) in Lundtofte, Denmark. There he had received his training as a pilot in Hærens Flyvertropper (the Army's Air Troops). Now he was a corporal and one of nine Danish pilots, who were on their way to Zürich in Switzerland to take part in a major international flying competition. Most European nations participated and a total of 140 planes and 400,000 spectators were present during the ten-day event. The Danes would be involved in three events: *formation flying* with five Fokker planes in which Carlo participated, *performance flying* with three Bulldog fighter planes which would compete in a 360 km long "Alpine flight", and *stunt flying*.

However, the road to Zürich was far from straight. Germany did not allow Danish military planes to fly over its territory in order not to risk revealing fortifications and illegal military fields. So, the flight plan meant a long detour over the Netherlands, Belgium and France. The journey started at 9.30 a.m. at Kastrup Airport outside Copenhagen. With bad weather approaching, the flight continued over southern Jutland and the North Sea, with a stopover in Amsterdam for refueling at 4 p.m.. At that time, it was forbidden for military planes flying over foreign territory to possess radios and, therefore, all communication was carried on with visual signs – movements of the head or hands in the open planes, flying in very close formation. Due to the weather, they were forced to fly near the ground in Holland. In Belgium, visibility became so bad that, despite flying at the level of Brussels' chimneys, they still missed the airport which was simply located on a field. When they discovered that they had reached the Franco-Belgian border, they turned around and eventually found Brussels' Airport. It was then time for an overnight stay (after a large reception with a sumptuous dinner and three kinds of wine). The next day the weather had cleared, and after a stopover in Nancy in France and a flight over the Vosges mountain range, Carlo and the other Danish pilots finally arrived at Zürich.

In Zürich a major drama awaited them. Carlo had just landed at the airport and was chatting with his companions. Suddenly an Italian squadron with nine planes, practicing stunt flying in formation, flew in over the airport at the height of 100 meters. The unusual part about this stunt was that the Italian planes flew on their backs – an impressive display, indeed. But a tragedy struck when the aircraft turned onto their right keel again. One of the Italian planes caught fire while flying at low speed. The Italian pilot, Sergeant Mario Sanzoni, attempted a steep wing glide, probably to avoid getting the flames in his face. He was thrown out of the plane and fell to the ground like a rock. He was seriously injured, suffering 23 bone fractures, and he died on the following day. It was the twenty-second pilot that this Italian squadron had lost in its attempts to perform stunt flying in formation. But, as Carlo later said, this was during Mussolini's time, and human life was not worth much.

The Danish formation team in Zürich, 1932. From left:
Sergeant H. Wolf, Lieutenant E. Lærum, Chief Officer
C. C. Larsen, Corporal J. Malmose, Corporal C. H. Sandqvist

Only a few days after this serious accident, it was time for the formation competitions. The five Danish Fokkers started in close formation under the leadership of Chief Officer C. C. Larsen with Carlo in an outermost position. Their program lasted twenty minutes and was executed with extremely high precision. There were two patterns "eight", single line, double line, staircase, and finally steep dive, all in close formation. The landing also took place in close formation. It was first-place prize for the Danish pilots! Their pride was great during the awards ceremony, when they received a large silver trophy and a diploma, 2,000 Swiss francs (a large sum at that time), individual engraved silver trophies and gold watches. Carlo felt an emotional shiver when the orchestra finally played the Danish anthem, "Kong Christian Stod ved Højen Mast"!

Carlo's lifetime prize trophies

During the home journey from Zürich to Copenhagen, new adventures await. The weather forecast offered a cloud level of only 300 meters over the Vosges mountain range. The five Fokkers started in formation – Carlo was again in the outermost position as number 5, the "most rotten place", according to his own words. As navigator he had Lieutenant Witterø, a 41-year-old who had been at the Flying School but had not been skilled enough to become a formation pilot. When the small group arrived at the Vosges, the clouds were covering the mountain peaks and the pilots could not fly onwards. C. C. Larsen led them back and forth in an attempt to find an opening in the cloud cover, but in vain. Then he led the group up through the clouds. Virtually no one had practised "blind" flying before, however, and their instruments consisted only of the compass, spirit level and airspeed indicator, no artificial horizon. It was all about following the neighbour's wing tip, so they flew even closer – even though they were already flying close. When they came up above the clouds, they discovered that there was a new cloud layer even higher up. Larsen then decided to go down through the clouds again. They had not yet crossed the mountain range, but flew back and forth along the mountains. A little later, they went up through the clouds a second time, and continued the ascent. At an altitude of 4,000 meters, they reached the top cloud layer, which they also entered. It now became extremely cold; they were after all in open cockpits. Carlo froze like a dog in his thin blue summer uniform. Another five hundred meters up and it started to snow. Suddenly the other four planes disappeared out of sight. Carlo and Witterø were alone in the snow clouds.

Carlo now decided to climb even higher. The clouds sealed so much that he couldn't even see the wing tips. Suddenly the engine stopped! Carlo automatically pushed the joystick for gliding. Panic struck, Witterø got up and shouted: "Let's jump, Sandqvist!". Not on your life, Carlo thought – jump over the Vosges? End up hanging from a tree? The Fokker glided quickly down, while the propeller spun slowly by the wind. When they came out of the top cloud layer, they saw a hole in the bottom layer. Carlo dove steeply toward the hole. If he could get through it, it might be possible to find a suitable stretch of ground to land on. No large field was required to land a Fokker. But, when he came out of the clouds at an altitude of 300 meters, he tried to start the engine, and it started immediately! The warmer air at lower altitude had caused the snow and ice in the carburettor to melt.

Now it was time to move on. Witterø and Carlo had previously agreed that if they got away from the others, they would go to Paris to hopefully spend a nice night there. But now their pride was too great to cancel the mission, and instead they went northwest using a car map, perhaps not the best tool. They had fuel for eight hours of flight, so that was no problem. One hour to the northwest and then straight north, Witterø calculated. Sooner or later there would be water beneath them: the English Channel, the North Sea, or simply Denmark. However, it was important to avoid Germany. They were indeed lost. But even though they passed occasional airports, it was too embarrassing to go down and ask, "Where are we?" After four or five hours, they finally saw the Rhine estuary at Rotterdam, and 20 minutes later, Amsterdam.

They landed in Amsterdam and asked: "Where are the other Danes?". Which other Danes, was the counter-question. And just while they stood there refuelling, the other four Danish Fokkers came rushing in at low altitude – they had seen Carlo's plane on the ground. Larsen, who was first in place, exclaimed loudly: "Sandqvist?! Are you still alive?" Carlo couldn't deny that, and he told his story. After spending the night in a hotel near the airport, the reunited squadron continued toward Denmark.

The welcome reception at Kastrup Airport in Copenhagen was magnificent. The news of the gold win in Zürich had already reached Denmark before the pilots themselves, and a large crowd had gathered to pay tribute to the winners and welcome them home. The five Fokkers flew in an excellent configuration over the airport and landed together in tight formation. The airmen and their navigators then had to endure being carried in "golden chair" over to Hærens Hangar for the welcome ceremony. The Chief of Aviation and the directors of the Ministry of War, the Aeronautical Society and the Danish Aviators gave lavish speeches. It all ended with the Danish authorities treating the winners to wine and wreath cake.

Chapter 2: Family Life, 1930 - 1935

In the luggage compartment of Carlo's Fokker, on the way home from Zurich, there was a package with somewhat unusual content. It was a beautiful cloth and some sewing accessories, which would become a dress – a gift to Lydia, Carlo's beloved. She was barely seventeen years old, but Carlo was deeply in love with her and she in him. They had already been keeping company for two years.

Carlo came from a large family that lived in a small two-room apartment in Copenhagen. His father, Oscar Sandqvist, was a carpenter and the son of two Swedish immigrants, who had come to Denmark from Sweden in the nineteenth century as children with their own families. Oscar was a very charming and popular man, especially amongst women who all fell for him. Carlo's mother, Agnes, was of Danish descent, quite strict, religious and determined. Carlo was thus half-Swedish, and he was often called "the Swede" by his friends. He was the oldest amongst siblings consisting of a two-year younger brother and four sisters. The brother, Børge, also became a flyer eventually.

Lydia also came from a large family. They lived in the Tingshuset in Frederiksværk, northern Zealand, where her father, Jørgen Damsholt, was a corrections officer and musician. Her mother, also called Lydia, was a music teacher who, among other things, played the organ in silent film screenings in the city's cinema. The daughter, Lydia, was the youngest of two boys and five girls. She was only six years old when her father died, and her mother had to shoulder the family responsibilities. Lydia blossomed into a beautiful young woman, and as the youngest in the crowd, she was both adulated and spoiled.

When Carlo was seventeen years old, he had a job as an office and errand boy for a store in Copenhagen, which specialised in women's clothing. One beautiful sunny day, when he had been sent by the owner to buy pastry, he was cycling past Søerne, the central lakes in Copenhagen. Suddenly he stopped. His attention had been directed upwards, up towards a growing rumble. There, about a thousand meters above Søerne, came three aeroplanes, flying in a stately formation. As if struck by a lightning flash, Carlo burst out: "That's it, that's what I want to be. I want to be an aviator! I want to be flying up there." But that was no easy goal. At that time, one could not become a pilot without becoming a military pilot or owning a fat bank account. The latter alternative was easy to exclude, and conscription normally took place at an age 21, – so it would be a long wait.

On his eighteenth birthday, Carlo was visited by his grandfather, a grumpy old man who used to bark at everything and everyone. "Well, good luck, Carlo," said the grandfather, "now you can become a soldier." "What? Soldier?", Carlo asked. "Yes, when you are 18, you can become a soldier." The very next day, Carlo was in Nyhavn, where the military had a reception, and requested immediate conscription, ready to defend Denmark. The officers looked at him with some scepticism. Carlo was slow in physical development and mostly resembled a fourteen-year-old boy. "Do you think you can carry a rifle?" one of the officers asked. "Yes, sir!" was the answer. "OK, into the infantry." And so began a military career that would end as captain in the Army Air Troops many years later.

During his recruitment period, spent at Kastellet in Copenhagen, Carlo became good friends with Knud Damsholt, Lydia's big brother. The two friends then entered the Corporal

School, where Carlo became best in a class of 55, while Knud was number 10. After that, both Carlo and Knud were stationed at Sandholm Camp where the two newly-baked corporals would begin training soldiers in the First Regiment. During the summer of 1930, they were moved to the Arresødal Camp where there was a high-quality shooting range. The Arresødal Camp lay on a hillside just outside Frederiksværk and had a magnificent view of the lake, Arresø. Everyone would live in four-man tents, shoot with sharp ammunition during the day and then dance with the girls at "Skovlyst" in Frederiksværk in the evenings. Great life for young men.

Since the Damsholt family lived in Frederiksværk, Knud thought it would be nice to invite Carlo home for dinner. Carlo was introduced to Knud's mother and two of the sisters, Lydia and Helga. Carlo's charm and good humour made him very popular in the family. The very next day, Lydia and Helga visited the Arresødal Camp and stood watching everything that happened in there. Carlo mentioned the two girls, – especially Lydia – whom they could see standing outside the camp, to his over sergeant who burst out: "What the hell, man! She is just a child!" And true enough, she was only fifteen years old, but Carlo had fallen for her.

There followed many cosy evenings at the Damsholt home in the Frederiksværk Courthouse. Lydia's mother quickly became fond of Carlo, and Lydia fell deeply in love with this handsome corporal. The family was very musical – the mother played the piano, Knud played the violin and so did Carlo. Often they would play together, and Lydia would accompany with her beautiful voice. And then, of course, there were all those dances at "Skovlyst" lasting long into the nights.

When the summer was over, the First Regiment returned to

the Sandholm Camp, and as winter arrived the regiment moved to Kastellet in Copenhagen. But Carlo was not happy – he wanted to be a pilot. Then, one day, a possible chance appeared: the Army Flying School needed seven students. Four hundred and thirty candidates applied, Carlo was one of them. At the end of all the tests, he was chosen as one of the seven! What happiness! In the spring of 1931, they happily arrived at the Flying School at Lundtofte airfield, full of expectations. But no aeroplanes awaited them there. Instead, the newly baked students were given shovels and told to smooth the airfield. The field was only a few hundred meters on each side but it had been completely undermined by moles. The surprised students, who had been leaders and were unaccustomed to physical work, quickly got blisters on their hands. Their consolation, however, was that when this mission was complete, the tempting aeroplanes would be waiting for them. But no! Instead there would be packing of parachutes, more parachutes, and even more parachutes. That procedure was naturally also essential to learn. Finally, after a long time, the students began flying. And thus Carlo became an aviator.

Carlo on his Harley-Davidson and Lydia
To be able to visit Lydia in Frederiksværk regularly, Carlo

bought a motorcycle, a Harley-Davidson. Knud would often accompany him on the trip. And Lydia got many local sunshine rides on the motorbike.

One early morning, a few months after the big success in Zürich, Carlo was on his way home from Frederiksværk on his dear Harley-Davidson. He was in a hurry to get to a meeting at Kløvermarken and broke the speed limit of 50 km/hour after passing the small village of Blovstrød. In the 1930s, Konge-vejen's highway surface consisted of square paving stones. After a curve, Carlo got the rising sun face-on, and he was blinded. Instead of stopping, or at least slowing down, he continued straight ahead in the middle of the road. A little further on, a medical doctor in his car was heading out onto Kongevejen from a side road, going in the same direction as Carlo. He heard the motorcycle, but was not sure if it would pass on the right or left side of his car – so he stopped the car obliquely in the middle of Kongevejen! A violent collision was inevitable. Carlo left the motorcycle and flew in a clear arch straight over the car. He landed on Kongevejen seven meters on the other side of the vehicle. The physician noticed how Carlo folded his arms around his head as he took off from the motorcycle, which undoubtedly saved his life. This was a routine reaction that Carlo's leader, C. C. Larsen, had ingrained in his pilots: "If you see that a crash is inevitable, up and protect your head with your arms!". Bloody and unconscious, Carlo was transported to the hospital by ambulance. He woke up briefly on the operating table and heard the doctor say to him: "Well, young man, you've probably been out riding on a motorcycle." "No, no, no, no!", Carlo replied, "Hell no, I've not been out riding a motorcycle" before he lost consciousness again. It took several days for him to regain consciousness.

After three weeks he was sent home from the hospital. However, a severe concussion would for the next couple of years prevent him from resuming aerobatic flight, which he had begun before the accident. But he was allowed to continue the normal flight, which would not have been permitted today.

Carlo became a flight instructor after his recovery, and eventually they were six or seven instructors, who also trained formation flight on the side. But they soon realized that this was not enough to entertain the large crowds, which came on flight days all over Denmark to see adventurous pilots. Sometimes 40,000 people would gather on the fields, so the natural next step was aerobatic flying in formation.

Formation flying in progress

One performance exercise consisted of flying in a column at 2,000 meters, with a few meters between the nose of one plane and the tail of the plane in front. The entire column would then dive vertically down towards the ground. The dive was terminated just above the ground. The aircraft, now only a few meters above the field, would then proceed up in a half-loop, which was called the "one-man-turn," a kind of half-roll, which ended in normal column flying.

At one time, the aerobatic column flew from Værløse to some engineering barracks outside Copenhagen, where there was a large practice field. Carlo was last in the column. At the end of the practice dive, the column rolled over onto its back. Carlo was a little slow this time in pulling on the joystick, and when he reached the top of the loop, with his head down, he did not have enough flying speed. As he tried to right keel, the plane slid down sideways. At this time, the formation column was only 100 meters above the ground! Carlo quickly pushed the joystick forward to increase the speed. He looked down to assess the risk and then noticed that he was looking straight down into the chimney of one of the two-story buildings of the engineering barracks. It was full of soot. "Good grief! That chimney needs to be cleansed", he thought. In the process of killing himself, his only concern was that the chimney below him could do with a chimney-sweep.

Friday, April 27, 1934.

A wedding took place between the nineteen-year-old Lydia and the twenty-four-year-old Carlo, and their families gathered for a big celebration in the Courthouse in Frederiksværk. Less than a year later, on March 12, 1935, their first son, Erik, was born in Gentofte, a suburb of Copenhagen. Carlo had by now resumed aerobatic flying, and he swept down and circled at low altitude just above the hospital where Lydia was lying with the newborn Erik in her arms. Her spontaneous, slightly envious reaction to Carlo's performance was: "It's easy for you to be flying up there, but here I lie and suffer". Nonetheless, the flight maneuvers certainly made an impression on both hospital staff and patients!

Four generations of Sandqvist: Otto, Oscar, Carlo and Erik

Chapter 3: Bromma Airport and Aalborg Airport, 1936 - 1939

Saturday, May 23, 1936

The King of Sweden, Gustaf V, had finished giving the inauguration speech for Bromma Airport. It was a miserable rainy day and another royalty, Prince Bertil, had just landed, becoming the first air passenger to Bromma. Sergeant Carlo Sandqvist, in his slow Tiger Moth, circled over the airport which was Stockholm's newest pride and Europe's first airport with four "hard" asphalt runways. Carlo chose a runway and landed after having completed his role in the big Nordic Cup flight competition, which had taken place in Sweden during Friday and Saturday (May 22 - 23).

It had all started on Tuesday, four days earlier, when 14 Danish military aircraft and their pilots and technicians had gathered at Kastrup Airport outside Copenhagen. It was not the first time a Nordic Cup flight competition had taken place. The first was held at Barkarby outside Stockholm on May 19 - 26, 1931, and the second at Kastrup on August 17 - September 2, 1934. But now, for the third Cup, it was Carlo's turn. The team's aircraft consisted of four new Fokker CVe, two older Fokker, one two-engine De Havilland Dragon, one Autogiro, and finally six relatively weak-engined and slow Tiger Moths. The pilots had navigators with them aboard the planes. Although Carlo had previously participated in other competitions, he was now given the inferior Tiger Moth – perhaps due to his previous competition experience. Having a slow aircraft was not the worst part, but a weak engine was definitely not desirable. The goal of the competition was not to be the fastest and first across the finish line, but to keep predetermined time intervals, navigate in unfamiliar territory, find flags laid out on the ground, and so on.

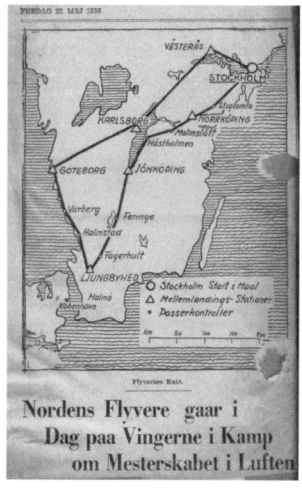

The Nordic Cup route,
according to a
Danish newspaper

Expectations were high in Denmark. The newspapers had full-page articles with portraits of the pilots. Now the Swedes would be shown who is best. However, why only four experienced competition pilots (of which Carlo was one) had been selected as participants while the others were unproven, was questioned. Another "injustice" was considered to be that the entire competition would take place over Swedish territory, which would then give the Swedes an advantage. But the Danish team received an honourable send-off in the presence of the Danish Commander-in-Chief, Lieutenant General With and the Chief of the Army Air Troops, Colonel Førslev. After the start in perfect weather, the Danes flew a short distance to Ljungbyhed in Skåne where Swedish customs control took place. After Ljungbyhed, the Danish pilots were to study the route of the Cup competition thoroughly, and now all the pilots flew individually at their own pace. The route on the first day took them up to Gothenburg, from there to Jönköping, and then to Norrköping for an overnight stay. Because of Bromma's upcoming inauguration, they were not allowed to land there until Wednesday. However, Norrköping put on a magnificent festive reception and superb dinner for the participants. The next day, the Danes flew over Västerås and finally landed on Bromma Airport among a severe jumble of aircraft, both in the air and on the ground. On Thursday, there was a final review of the scope and rules of the Nordic Cup, and the leader of the Danish team, Captain Bjarkov, issued his final order with half a smile: "Everyone completes the competition, no one gives up!". He was perhaps referring to the deteriorating weather conditions, which had now begun to threaten the event.

On Friday, the competition started under dense threatening clouds, hanging low over Bromma. As seen on a map in a Danish newspaper, the route would encompass landings in Norrköping, Jönköping, Ljungbyhed and Gothenburg. From Gothenburg, the route turned back to Jönköping where an overnight stay would take place. (Contrary to the slightly erroneous Danish newspaper map, there would be no stopover in Karlsborg). On the second day of the competition, there was

Excerpt from Carlo's logbook

Carlo's photo of Taberg near Jönköping

Inauguration of Bromma Airport.
The Danish aircraft can be seen in the distance
on the far right

to be a landing in Västerås before the final lap to Bromma on Bromma's grand opening day. Carlo's logbook shows that he flew the whole route in the miserable weather at 600 meters. Quite often the clouds forced the pilots down to only a few hundred meters above the ground, and in some cases the clouds covered the peaks of the hills of the highlands. The rain poured down during much of the competition, which was less than fun in these open planes. The sun didn't show itself until late on the inauguration day. In total, 43 aircraft from Sweden, Denmark, Norway and Finland managed to complete the competition. First and second place went to the Swedes, a Dane did come in third place. However, it was not Carlo. With his Tiger Moth, he had to settle for a modest 39th place – "next time I want a Fokker", he thought. But all the Danes passed the finish line, and that was the most important thing. In the evening there was a grand reception in the Stockholm City Hall.

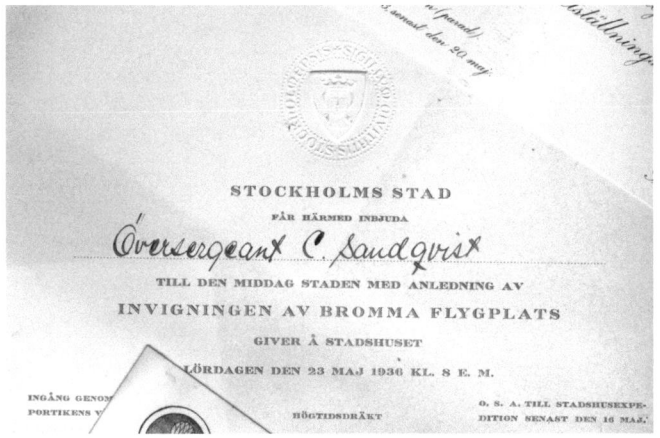

Carlo's invitation to the reception in the Stockholm City Hall

Carlo's job in the Air Troops was seasonal. Like many of the other Danish military pilots, he was laid off during the winters. He had to look for other jobs during that part of the year – a situation that was not sustainable in the long run. But he didn't want to give up his flying. Now he was lucky. A new Danish airport was to be inaugurated, and this event would prove to be essential for his future. Aalborg Airport was inaugurated on Sunday, May 29, 1938, – a simple grassy field of only 119 hectares in the northern part of Jutland. A car dealer, Magnus Christiansen, in Hobro, a town about 60 km south of Aalborg, wanted to start a flying school at the new Aalborg Airport, but he did not know much about flying.

Carlo, in front of the flying school's aeroplanes
at Aalborg Airport

After six years as flight instructor in the Army's Air Troops, Carlo transferred to the Army Reserves and now became instructor and head of the new flying school. On October 11, he flew Magnus Christiansen's first aircraft, which was purchased in Copenhagen, to Aalborg. It was a two-seater De Havilland

Hornet Moth with an enclosed cockpit – "a great plane", according to Carlo. In the passenger seat, sat Lydia with a slightly feverish three-year-old Erik in her lap. The flight from Copenhagen had been very bumpy due to inclement weather. The trip took two and a half hours, more than twice as long as usual. Lydia, who was pregnant in the second month with the couple's second child, had been airsick most of the trip. However, she did recover somewhat just before the city's newspaper photographers welcomed the little family at the new airport in Aalborg.

The new flying school was completed shortly thereafter by the purchase of two new Piper Cubs. Within about a month, Carlo had trained Aalborg's first private pilot, and during the first half of 1939, another six of Carlo's students received their flying certificates.

A week before Carlo and his family moved from Copenhagen to Aalborg, he visited his parents. During a short walk, Carlo's father said to him: "Carlo, now you are going to Aalborg. Now you have to watch out for the girls up there, they are really dangerous." Carlo then replied: "Don't worry about that, Dad, I'm happily married, right? – We have Erik, and a new child is on its way. Nothing will happen." But, something did happen!

One morning a few months later, Carlo was on his way out the door of Magnus Christiansen's Aalborg car branch and about to get into one of Magnus' cars, which he used daily to get to the airport. Facing him suddenly in the doorway was a young 18-year-old girl, who had come to visit her friend, Magnus' secretary. They stood there looking at each other. The girl smiled. "Something happened inside me, like an explosion, I fell in love. Right then and there", Carlo said much later. At the same time, the secretary came running and told Carlo that the girl was Miss Vibæk, Elsa Vibæk, her best friend. They exchanged a few words, after which Carlo got into the car and drove to the airport. Nothing was the same after that. For a long time, Carlo had realized that Lydia really "wasn't right for him," as his mother had warned him before they got married. There was no real contact with Lydia when Carlo tried to talk to her. With Elsa it was completely different. They were on the same wavelength, could talk about everything, enjoy themselves. Elsa became Carlo's mistress. And on June 1, 1939, Lydia gave birth to Carlo's second son, Aage.

Elsa, in front of the main building on Aalborg Airport

Chapter 4: Beginning of World War II, Værløse Airport, 1940

Friday, September 1, 1939.

Carlo was sitting with some friends in Ritz Safari, one of Aalborg's most excellent restaurants, when he was reached by the alarming news that Germany was attacking Poland. Lydia was home with the two little boys. Two days later, at 11.45 a.m. on Sunday morning, it was reported on the radio that England and France had declared war on Germany, and the Second World War was a fact. A large number of rules, restrictions and aviation regulations were quickly introduced in Denmark, and civil aviation became more and more difficult. Carlo, now a lieutenant in the Reserves, applied a few months later for regular military service and was immediately summoned to the Army's Air Troops again. So in early 1940, Carlo left Aalborg Airport and was stationed at Værløse Flyveplads, north of Copenhagen, where the the Army's Air Force Troops resided.

The Danish Army's Air Troops at Værløse Airport in 1937

Together with Lydia and the two boys, Carlo moved into a small one-storeyed villa in Farum, near Værløse. It didn't take long before Elsa followed him to Copenhagen, and they continued their secret relationship. However, Carlo suffered greatly from a bad conscience, and he tried to end it all. Elsa went into despair, and Carlo felt miserable. So in the end, they gave in to their feelings and carried on as before.

On the international front, England threatened to invade Norway in order to prevent the transport of Swedish iron ore from Narvik in northern Norway to Germany, and the establishment of German submarine bases in the Norwegian fjords. An English fleet presence in southern Norway would also be able to block the sea route to the Baltic Sea. Germany wanted to prevent this English plan by an invasion of Norway. However, the German aircraft could not fly the long distance from northern Germany to southern Norway without a stopover somewhere for refueling. A quick look at a map clearly shows that Aalborg Airport in northern Jutland was critical as a German stepping stone to Norway, and this fact was also the most important motivation for Germany's imminent occupation of Denmark. Also, Aalborg Airport was well placed for monitoring large parts of the North Sea.

At the outbreak of the war in 1939, Denmark quickly declared its neutrality. In a speech in January, 1940, the Danish Prime Minister, T. H. Stauning, expressed the view that Denmark was incapable of following other countries' examples of creating a convincing defence, even if there was a wish to do so. This was interpreted by both friends and enemies as though Denmark would offer *no* defence if attacked. But confusion prevailed because the Danish General Command had previously adopted a policy that a direct attack on Danish territory would be repelled immediately, "using all available means" without waiting for new commands. The Prime Minister followed up his speech by making it clear that the country's forces would obviously be deployed to stave off an attack on Denmark's neutrality. Despite warnings coming to Copenhagen from various sources in Berlin during the first week of April 1940 – that a German attack on Denmark was planned for the following week – no special precautionary measures were taken in Denmark. The Danish Air Troops were all stationed exclusively at Værløse Airport. They consisted of 92 aircraft, mainly fighter and reconnaissance aircraft, of which one third were in the repair shop. Of the 62 functional aeroplanes, only seven were reasonably modern, namely Fokker D.XXI. These planes were however hopelessly inferior to the German Messerschmitt 109 and 110. The other aircraft were old types such as Fokker CV, O machine, Gloster Gauntlet and Tiger Moth.

German Heinkel 111 attacks Denmark

In northern Germany, on April 9, 1940, an armada of one thousand aircraft had gathered and was ready to take off against

Denmark and Norway. History's first parachute attack would be carried out against Aalborg Airport to secure this stepping stone, where the German aircraft could then refuel before flying on towards Norway. But first, the Danish Air Troops would have to be destroyed.

Tuesday, April 9, 1940. Carlo woke up early in the morning around 3 a.m. lying in his camp bed in a barrack on Værløse Airport. Outside, some squadrons were swiftly driving out of the camp. A few days earlier, the camp had been put on high alert, and all leaves had been cancelled. Young Danish fighter pilots were patrolling the Danish west coast in old-fashioned aircraft which were only half as fast as the German aeroplanes – ready to defend Denmark with "all available means". The aircraft did have 9-mm recoil rifles in the nose – but there was no ammunition for the guns. "So, your choice of attack was to either place yourself in the path of the oncoming enemy plane, or else fly right into it," Carlo had thought. But Carlo was a flight instructor, not a fighter pilot, so he stayed in bed a little longer. Suddenly all hell broke loose from heavy machine guns. Carlo got out of bed in a hurry, on with his uniform and quickly up to the administration building. There were already a lot of pilots here – the head of the fighter and security section, Lieutenant Colonel Bjarkov, Carlo's former boss, C. C. Larsen, and many of Carlo's former flying students. Suddenly a window was opened on the second floor and the head of the Air Troops, Colonel Førslev, appeared in shirtsleeves without uniform and shouted down to the assembly: "Bjarkov, do something. Do something! Before I come down. And put up a defence of the camp! "

Bjarkov reacted immediately and quickly distributed tasks to different groups: "Lieutenant Sandqvist, take the corporal school and defend the east side of the camp!" The corporal school consisted of 22 mechanics, who had received only six weeks of military training. Also, Carlo got two second lieutenants at his disposal. When it came to weapons, Carlo had his old drum pistol which could shoot "10 meters, if the wind came from the rear", and the corporals received rifles from 1889, "the world's best rifles, they could hit anything. They were so long that, no matter his distance, the enemy would still have the rifle's nozzle right in his stomach." Carlo knew that there were 20-mm cannons in the camp's weapons storage, but they were not taken out because "you were not allowed to upset the Germans and make them angry"! Thus Carlo marched off with his "giant" force out to the east side of the camp. On the way, he met his brother, Børge, who was also stationed at Værløse. "Well, here we go off to war", Carlo said to Børge, "I have been trained for aeroplanes, and now I am going to war as an infantry lieutenant instead".

The German attack on Værløse Airport was initiated with about ten Messerschmitt 110 fighter planes at half-past six in the early dawn. A total of thirty German aircraft participated in the attack. It was only half an hour earlier that the camp had been informed of the German violation of the southern border, and that the attack on Denmark was in full swing. Værløse's flight squadrons should therefore immediately be relocated to different Danish airports (somewhat late, one might suspect), and some aircraft had already been pulled out of the hangars and stood with their engines running. One aeroplane, a Fokker C V, with Lieutenant Godtfredsen as pilot and Lieutenant Brodersen as observer, both of whom were Carlo's former flying students, had begun to take off at the same time as the first Messerschmitt planes flew over the airport. The Danes barely

reached an altitude of 50 meters before a high-speed Messerschmitt came in from behind and opened fire. Brodersen answered the fire with his rifle, but Godtfredsen was hit, and the
Fokker immediately plunged towards the ground. Brodersen
tried to jump, but his parachute could not unfold in time. The
two pilots, dying in an exploding fireball, were the only ca-
sualties at Værløse that morning, since the Germans had been
given strict orders not to attack people unnecessarily and only
destroy equipment. Of the 45 functional Danish aircraft, 11
were totally destroyed, and 14 were so badly damaged that they
were unusable.

What did this attack on Værløse Airport look like from a
German horizon? Early in the dawn of April 9, the commander
of the German flight unit Zerstörergeschwader 1 ZG-1, Hauptmann Falck, had led his two squadrons of two-engine Messerschmitt 110:s, starting from Barth in northern Germany, out
over the Baltic Sea towards Værløse in Denmark. To avoid de-
tection, they flew very low, about 10 meters above sea level,
towards the coast of Zealand. Here they climbed up to 500
meters in order to attack the main force of the Danish Air
Troops at Værløse with the rising sun in the back. Their task
was to destroy as many Danish aircraft on the ground as possible and prevent them from getting into the air. After that, the
squadrons would join and support Kampgeschwader 4's de-
monstration flight over Copenhagen. Finally, they would turn
towards Aalborg Airport in Northern Jutland, to join the bulk of
the German invasion air armada.

Danish aeroplanes at Værløse Airport after the German attack (Photos: Air Force Historical Collection, FLYHIS)

When Hauptmann Falck came in over Værløse, he saw that many aircraft were lined up on the ground with their engines running. One plane was about to start. He quickly dived behind the starting plane and fired both his guns and cannons. The Danish plane burst into flames and immediately crashed into to the field. Falck pulled up his Messerschmitt, banked and looked back down at the airport. Smoke and flames were rising up from a large number of Danish aircraft. He attacked again. However, during his third attack, his aircraft was hit by the feeble Danish defence and one of his engines stopped. He was now forced to return to Germany where he changed planes. After that, he could fly on to Aalborg Airport, which by now was under complete German control.

German pilots and aircraft at Aalborg Airport on April 9, 1940
(Photo: Aalborg City Archive)

Meanwhile, Carlo, with his small defending unit, lay on the eastern side of Værløse Airport and waited, and waited, and waited. After a couple of hours, a message came that King Christian X had issued an order that all fighting against the Germans should be stopped! Denmark had been occupied. The next day, three German officers arrived in a Fieseler-Storch aircraft at Værløse. Colonel Førslev accompanied the three officers, impressive in their uniforms and long blue coats. Førslev was pale with a horrible facial expression. Both Carlo and Børge were of a similar mood, and the whole camp felt the same. In the evening the Danish flag, Dannebrog, was lowered. On April 25, the German Swastika was hoisted; the Germans had taken over the camp. Carlo and the Flying School were moved to the nearby Skovlunde School. On the German order, all reserve officers were laid off. In an attempt to retain some regular officers, the Danes arranged a Captains' course. Both Carlo and Børge were accepted at this course. The Captains' course ended in December, and then Carlo and Børge were also laid off and sent home.

Chapter 5: Work for the Germans – in Germany 1941 - 1942, at Aalborg Airport 1942 - 1944

January, 1941.

It was a brutal winter and very cold. Carlo was now unemployed. No matter how hard he tried, there were no means of sustenance to be found anywhere. Without income, life was very difficult for the small family with Lydia and the two little sons. During the Captain's course, Carlo had received a low monthly salary which was not big enough for any saving. After the course, there was no income at all. Neither was there any government support to be had. It was not unusual for oatmeal to be served several times a day. Carlo and Erik often went out into the nearby woods to collect firewood for the stove.

Carlo became more and more desperate. Finally, he went to the Minister of Public Works and presented his new untenable situation, which had arisen after serving Denmark in the military for over twelve years. Carlo stated that he was willing to take any job. After a long reflection, the Minister said: "Go to Germany and get a job in a large machine factory." Carlo objected that he had no idea about a factory worker's duties, but the Minister insisted that the Germans would accept Carlo because he spoke German fluently. It would be a simple matter to go to the German employment office in Copenhagen and present himself as a machine operator. And in Germany, Carlo should then keep his eyes open and report back to the Minister. But under no circumstance should Carlo mention that this proposal came from the Minister. However, there would be no support from the ministry, financial or otherwise. Instead, the Minister issued an official letter to Carlo, regretting that he had been unable to help him. Among Danes generally, this Minister was considered to be German-friendly, but Carlo suspected that the Minister "was playing both sides". After the war, Carlo would be rewarded. That did not happen, the Minister died.

There was no problem getting a job in Germany. Carlo was hired in February at Junkers aircraft factory in Köthen, Anhalt, 100 km from Berlin. Here, Junkers manufactured aircraft engines which were then sent to the large assembly plants in Dachau. Elsa also applied for a job in Germany and was quickly employed by "AG" in Berlin. Carlo had decided to tell Lydia that their marriage was over when he returned home on his first leave. He thought that it might be easier for her to accept such a decision after a longer separation. Elsa had travelled to Berlin and from there, unfortunately, wrote a letter addressed to Carlo's home address. It arrived shortly after he had left for Köthen and Lydia opened the letter. It was like being struck by lightning! She was devastated. Her two sons were placed in an orphanage. After a little over a month, Lydia's brother, Harald, and his wife took care of Erik, but nobody wanted a two-year-old, so Aage had to remain by himself in the orphanage.

Meanwhile, Carlo had arrived at the Junkers engine factory in Köthen. The foreman, an engineer, carefully examined Carlo's hands, and, with a skeptical "Hmmmm", placed him as a fine-grinder. Carlo quickly learned the fine-grinding profession and began grinding components for the gearbox, which sat between the engine and the propeller. The engine had a speed of 3000 rpm, while the propeller should turn at 1500 rpm. The grinding of the gear should be performed with an accuracy of one micrometer. A little too much grinding and the propeller could be shattered later in operation. This fact gave Carlo the idea of occasionally giving the diamond grinder a little extra pressure.

He did not dare that too often but probably did cause some failures. One day, Engineer Bendtman came to him and asked him, why he was working there as a regular machine operator while he had a rank as a Danish aviation officer. The engineer had talked to Colonel Udet, aviator hero in World War I, who was now head of the German flight testing of new aircraft in Dessau. Udet wanted Carlo as test pilot and would give him rank as Hauptmann. Carlo was strongly upset by this proposal and refused. He did not want to wear a German uniform. It was bad enough that he was compelled to work in Germany in order to support his family back in Denmark. Bendtman found Carlo's objections incomprehensible and tried to persuade him several times. But in vain.

The months went by. The trips to Berlin to be with Elsa became cumbersome, and Elsa soon moved to Köthen where she also managed to find a job. In August it was time for the first holiday back in Denmark. For the first time, Carlo discovered that Aage was in an orphanage and had been there for half a year. Carlo immediately went to the orphanage, bringing a toy with him that he had bought on the way. The children were all out in the yard, and there he saw Aage strolling along the wire fence, hand in hand with a child's nurse. "Never in my life have I seen such a sad and abandoned expression in a child's face," thought Carlo. Aage did not recognise his father and was utterly uninterested in the toy. Carlo went right away to the superintendent and informed her that he was removing Aage from the orphanage at once. That was illegal, the superintendent objected, because it was the child's mother who had placed him there. Carlo's answer was unambiguous: "I don't give a damn if it's the King himself who has placed him here, I am Aage's father, and I'm bloody well taking him with me

NOW!"

Carlo, Aage and Elsa in Gug

Carlo, Elsa and the "kidnapped" Aage then went to Aalborg, to Elsa's parents who had a vegetable farm in Gug, seven km south of Aalborg. Carlo and Elsa told Elsa's parents that they wanted to get married and then go back to their jobs in Germany – would Elsa's parents be willing to take care of Aage? After fifteen minutes of private discussion, they said "Yes!" Lydia and Carlo were divorced on September 24, and shortly thereafter Lydia married Carl Kjær, a restaurant owner in Copenhagen. He was willing to accept Erik but did not want Aage also. He, therefore, prevented Lydia from taking back Aage with help of the long arm of the law. On December 20, Carlo and Elsa were married, and then they went back to Germany. Aage stayed behind in Gug with his new "Grandma" and "Grandpa".

Aage with his new Grandma and Grandpa

January, 1942.

The second stay in Germany was less successful. Carlo and Elsa still had their jobs. But Carlo's entire fine-grinding engine department eventually moved to Czechoslovakia, and he was made to grind cylinders instead, a disgusting and dirty job that he did not like. He requested another job, which was denied. Then he began staying away from work. It didn't take long for the Work Police to come and pick him up (at five o'clock in the morning). After a short time in prison, he was summoned to the Chief of the Work Police, a colonel in the SS. Carlo gave the colonel a proper scolding for treating a Danish guest worker in this way. That seemed to sink in, for Carlo was freed, but he still had to return to his dirty work. Now, it didn't take long for Carlo to start missing work again, and, sure enough, there was the Work Police back to pick him up – still early in the morning. This time, the SS colonel threatened to send Carlo to a labour camp if he continued to be obstinate. Carlo gave the colonel a new thorough scolding. He knew that there was something strange about the Germans: if you showed them that you were not afraid of them but acted loud and commandeering, then you could accomplish a great deal. Carlo ended his verbal attack by informing the colonel that he now wanted to go back home to Denmark – he had been in Germany for three quarters of a year during 1942 and thus officially did not need to renew his employment contract. He was in Germany of his own free will, and this was no way to treat a Danish officer. He wanted to go home to Denmark NOW! Carlo was also supported by Engineer Bendtman, the foreman at the Junkers factory who had been very satisfied with Carlo's performance. Finally, the SS colonel yielded, and Carlo was freed. He got his papers in order and, together with Elsa, could go back home to Denmark.

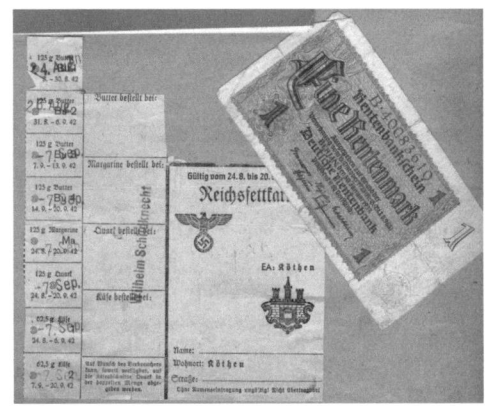

Carlo's German rationing stamps and money

Back in Aalborg, Carlo managed to get a job out at Aalborg Airport, which the Germans had taken over. He obtained this, thanks to his aviation background and his employment in

Germany, and because he spoke fluent German. The Germans allowed Danes at the airport: Danish construction workers, architects, and engineers. Carlo was placed in the airport engineering office. Later on, he also became an "alert-report leader" in the Air Notification Service at the Danish Civil Aviation Authority's Command Center, which was also located at the airport. The Civil Aviation Authority was a Danish authority, established in May, 1938, as a response to the growing unrest in Europe. The Command Center would monitor the air traffic over the country and also issue early warnings of impending air attacks. After the German occupation of Denmark, the German Wehrmacht became responsible for the observation posts, which reported to the Air Notification Service, which in turn warned affected areas in Denmark. The Service was active 24 hours a day with different shifts, and each shift consisted of one leader (Carlo was one) as well as a dozen telephone girls.

Aalborg Airport before the war (Photo: Aalborg City Archive)

Aalborg Airport had changed a lot since Carlo last worked there. April 9, 1940, when the Germans dropped their parachute troopers over Aalborg Airport, was the beginning of the end of the "lawn" status of the airport. The hundreds of German aircraft, that landed on the "lawn" that day, plowed up the field and made a mess. The aeroplanes got stuck in the mud, and an unbelievable traffic chaos ensued, with multiple collisions on the ground as a result. That situation would change quickly, though. Only ten days later, the German engineer, Bauleiter Karl Bruns, arrived at Aalborg Airport with large-scale plans. First, the airport area was expanded from 119 hectares to 3,056 hectares. The culturally valuable mansion, Rödslet, dating back to the 15th century, was quickly levelled. The same was true of 250 farms that were in the way! Barracks, capable of housing 2,200 Germans, were quickly constructed. Within three months, there were a 1,800-meter long, 80-meter wide runway in concrete, and very soon another concrete runway of 1,800 meters and a third of 1,400 meters. The three runways lay in a triangle which permitted flight under all wind conditions. Taxi lanes for the aircraft were laid out, 36 hangars were built, and 60 bunkers with concrete walls about half a meter in thickness were erected. Countless barracks for staff housing and entertainment, such as cinema and theatre, etc. were built. Railway tracks and streets, with names such as General Wolff-Strasse, Immelmann-Strasse, Göring-Strasse, were constructed. The airport was surrounded by defence cannons and air defence artillery. Fliegerhorst Aalborg West was now established as Northern Europe's largest airport and garrison. The expansion and remodelling of the airport continued throughout the war. The airport was Northern Jutland's largest work place with up to 16,000 Danes employed at various times. The cost was no problem for the

Germans. They forced the Danish National Bank to pay the bill of 1.1 billion Danish kroner, perhaps 25 billion in today's monetary value. This was Carlo's new place of work.

Aalborg Airport after the German expansion
(Photo: Aalborg Airport)

In the engineering office and the Air Notification Service, Carlo had access to both architectural drawings of bunkers and other buildings, as well as aerial photographs. These he micro-photographed in secret, and the results were sent to England. At the same time, he tried to form a resistance group in Aalborg, not an easy task in the autumn of 1942.

Nine out of ten persons, whom he tried to recruit for the group, said no, most in consideration of their families. Some were not sure where the war was heading. But, eventually, he succeeded in organizing a small resistance group, one of the first in the Aalborg area. The goal of these groups was that, in the event of an Allied invasion, or when a German defeat was looming, the groups would emerge from their underground activities and take up the fight against the Germans. The groups would, therefore, prepare for such situations. However, they were not intended for committing sabotage.

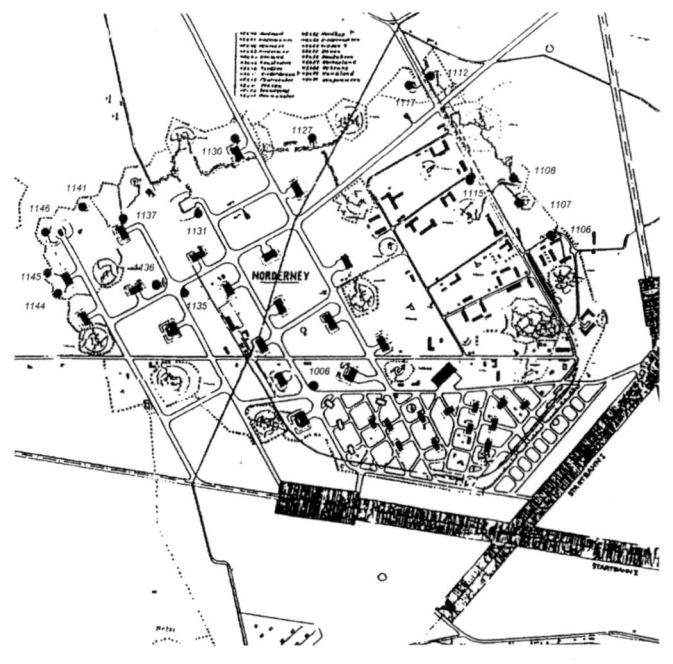

German map of part of Aalborg Airport
(Air Station Aalborg, A. C. Johansen)

Carlo's resistance activities were focused on training the groups in the use of weapons, and he had a good background for this job through his military career. He obtained weapons from Britain through parachute drops from British aircraft on various occasions in northern Jutland. They consisted of hand-

GEHEIME KOMMANDOSACHE !

Nr.: A 50 m 15/ -12. Ausfertigung

Geheime Kommandofache

Flugplatz Aalborg - West

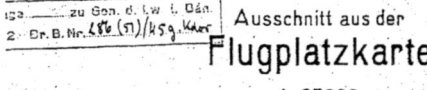

133 ...... zu Gen. d. Lw. i. Dän.
2. Dr. B. Nr. 486 (57)/459. KАer

Ausschnitt aus der

Flugplatzkarte

1 : 25000

Rechtweisender Kurs der Anfluggrundlinie 239°

Lfd. Nr.	Punktbezeichnung	Rechtwinklige Koordinaten		Geographische Koordinaten		Entfernung von R.B.P.	Bemerkungen
		Rechts	Hoch	Länge λ	Breite φ		
1	RBP.	169 035,1	432 899,2	9 51 53,8	57 05 33,4		Stein
2	P. (1400 m)	170 111,1	433 535,4	9 53 03,3	57 05 54,4	1250	feste Anlage
3	LSS.	167 519,7	432 003,4	9 50 30,8	57 05 04,1	1780	" "
4	HEZ. (1400m)	169 723,7	433 306,4	9 52 40,4	57 05 47,0	800	" "
5	YEZ.	172 313,9	434 837,7	9 65 13,6	57 06 38,3	3809	" "
6	T.	170 526,2	433 840,7	9 53 33,7	57 06 04,3	1850	Pfahl
7	Fu 0.16	170 886,5	433 993,4	9 53 48,9	57 06 09,3	2150	"
8	Fu. 5Z.	169 918,1	434 520,2	9 52 33,3	57 06 25,0		feste Anlage
9	Fu. B.St.	169 364,8	433 957,9	9 52 19,7	57 05 04,1		" "
10	WG.	170 250,4	433 332,5	9 53 11,5	57 05 47,7		mat.

Mißweisung u. Nadelabweichung RBP für Mitte 1945

Windhäufigkeitsdiagramm

Rollfeldbeschaffenheit:

ebene sandige Ackerfläche, angeschl.
Grasnarbe, feucht, teils drainiert.
Wiederherstellungsarbeiten daran
ständig erforderlich- Grundwasser
0,60 m unter Gelände.

jährliche Änderung - - 0,6°

Ausschnitt aus top.Karte
1 : 25000
Jägergradnetzzahl
für R.B.P = 05 Ost - Nord HU 5 7 e

Beobachtungsort: Aalborg Ost

N

Zeichenerklärung:

---- im Bau ---- geplant
verstärkte Randleuchte
Dreipunkt Randleuchte.
Einpunkt Randleuchte.

Flughindernisse Höhe ü. RBP.
befeuert
unbefeuert

------ Dez. - Febr.   ------ Juni - Aug.
------ März - Mai   ------ Sept. - Nov.
------ Jahresmittel   ------ Σ ± 5m/sek.

M. 1cm = 7.5 %

Kommandierender General der Deutschen Luftwaffe in Dänemark
(II. Fliegerkorps)
Abt. I Mess.

Secret German airport map instructions for Aalborg Airport
(Air Station Aalborg, A. C. Johansen)

grenades, pistols and machine guns, which he kept in a suitcase at home in the apartment on Bornholmsgade in Aalborg. It was also in his home that the training of the resistance groups and handling of these weapons took place. When the weapons were not in use, the suitcase, containing them, was hidden outdoors in a small space between the balcony and the house wall. After the defeat of the Germans at Stalingrad in February, 1943, when many Danes now began to understand that the Germans might lose the war, it was no longer so difficult to recruit new resistance members.

During a year and a half, the operation went smoothly without any problems. But then one day late in the winter of 1944, the Germans arrested one of Carlo's resistance members. It was Peter Jakob, the son of an important landowner in Gug, who for a while had been carelessly walking around and bragging about being a part of a secret organization. Carlo immediately went underground. But contacts from inside the prison, where Peter Jakob had been placed, informed him that a much milder suspicion against Peter Jakob was the cause of his arrest. In the vernacular, a "secret organization" had eventually transformed into the possession of "a secret transmitter", which was not such a serious crime as participation in a resistance movement. After three weeks, Carlo felt safe again and returned to his job at Aalborg Airport. But that turned out to be a big mistake.

Chapter 6: German Concentration Camp in Horserød, 1944

Thursday, April 20, 1944.

Adolf Hitler's Birthday. A day to remember for Carlo, but not because of Hitler, not directly anyway. At home in the apartment on Bornholmsgade, Elsa had just started cleaning up after breakfast. Aage was sitting on a couch in the living room with one leg resting on a pillow, his foot wrapped in bandages. A week earlier, he had undergone a minor operation for a blister caused by a wooden clog. Suddenly, there was a loud banging on the front door. In rushed two German soldiers in full military dress with helmets and rifles, followed by a Danish civilian collaborator. They were looking for Carlo and now searched the apartment recklessly, overturned furniture, tore out drawers and threw the contents on the floor, emptied bookshelves and cabinets. One of the Germans even stuck his bayonet deep into a glass jar with pickled cucumbers, which Elsa's mother had brought from the farm in Gug just a few days earlier – no hand grenades there. Aage followed the drama from the sofa with eyes wide open. However, the hiding place on the balcony was not investigated and the suitcase with weapons was left undiscovered. The intruders left the apartment as quickly as they had arrived. Elsa yelled at the Dane before she slammed the door shut behind them: "You're going to hang from a lamp post on Nytorv after the war" – (and that's exactly what happened).

Balcony on Bornholmsgade

At the same time out at Aalborg Airport – there the Germans had better luck. It was nine o'clock, and Carlo was about to install himself at his desk at the Air Notification Service, while the dozen-or-so telephone girls were also changing to a new team. Carlo always had an unsecured loaded pistol lying. "If they come to get me, I'm damn well not going to be taken without at least a shot being fired," was his plan. But just then, in all the confusion surrounding the change of teams, there had been no time to put the gun in place. Suddenly, four Gestapo men stood in front of him with their guns drawn. He had no other choice than to follow them to the Gestapo headquarters in Aalborg, the High School Home. Here sat another Gestapo man, who then began to interrogate Carlo. Carlo now had to be careful because he did not know what he was suspected of having done. It could be anything from handing out illegal magazines, espionage at the airport, activity as a weapons instructor, all the way to organising a resistance group. He started by denying all. The Gestapo man was not impressed and informed Carlo that they already knew everything because Peter Jakob had not kept his mouth shut. Now it became a matter of figuring out how much Peter Jakob had revealed. Eventually, Carlo realised that Peter Jakob had only mentioned his first and only meeting in Carlo's home, where he had been given weapons instructions. He had not mentioned that there were six other people in the group present, and he did not know that Carlo also instructed other groups in Aalborg. Carlo then presented his backstop emergency lie: he had made preparations for fighting the Communists if the Germans were to leave Denmark, and he needed Peter Jakob's help in this. But that story did not hold water with the Gestapo man. However, the Germans had no incriminating evidence. After that, Carlo was taken down into the basement – with a gun in his back. "What is going to happen now?" Carlo thought. Gestapo's torture methods were well known and right now he did not feel courageous. He struggled to keep his self-control. In the basement, Carlo was relieved of his uniform, his engraved gold watch from Zürich and his King's badge. Nothing more happened. The watch and the King's badge were sent to Elsa as proof that the Germans had now arrested him. The entire resistance movement in Aalborg immediately went under-ground because Carlo knew the names of most of the members. It took a long time for them to resurface. Later, one could read in the Aalborg Stiftstidene (the city's leading daily newspaper) that the Danish Civil Aviation Authority had hired a new alert-report leader in the Command Center and the District Com-mand in Aalborg, replacing Lieutenant Sandqvist who had been incapacitated due to special circumstances. Censorship meant that the newspaper was not allowed to write that the Gestapo had taken Carlo. But Danes understood.

Carlo was then transferred to the prison on Kong Hans Street. Elsa was naturally miserable and, already on the next day, she tried to get into the prison to see Carlo. She took a portion of yellow pea soup with her and a piece of soap. Since there was no-one to take care of Aage, he went along with her. The guard did not allow Elsa to go up to Carlo but suggested that the almost five-year-old Aage could carry the yellow pea soup by himself up to his father in the prison cell. There was no way that Elsa would permit this, and so the pea soup and soap were handed over to the guard. The yellow pea soup eventually reached Carlo but had spoiled in the meantime.

Early on the third day, a new Gestapo man came to inter-rogate Carlo, accompanied by an interpreter, a Danish collaborator. But Carlo didn't need an interpreter. The new hearing lasted all day, but Carlo revealed nothing new. Five days later, a covered truck left the prison. Under the cover sat Carlo and some other prisoners, and they were now on their way to the German concentration camp in Horserød, on Zealand. After a long drive, the truck stopped outside Odense on Funen. The prisoners were ordered down from the truck and made to stand in a circle to pee. "It's not easy to piss when you have such a bunch of soldiers with machine guns standing right behind you", Carlo thought, before being forced up on the truck again for the remainder of the trip.

Near the end of April, 1944, Horserød's concentration camp consisted of two parts, Camp 1 and the newly started Camp 2. Camp 1 was now full of 700 prisoners, its Danish leader was Captain P. M. Digmann. Carlo was interned in Camp 2 as prisoner number 20. Camp 2 had two large barracks and each building had two halves with a hall in the middle and long corridors extending from the sides. Every day new prisoners arrived and Camp 2 grew rapidly. The German commander was a handsome Sergeant Wassermann, who looked tough but actually was a very nice person on the inside. One day, he stopped directly in front of Carlo, who was in the front row of the daily lineup. He looked Carlo straight in the eyes and demanded loudly if anyone present could speak German. One thing led to another, and soon Carlo was the leader of Camp 2 with a small staff of six men, which would keep order of the 175 prisoners in the two large barracks. Carlo's staff consisted of, among others, P. Federspiel who after the war became Danish Minister of Special Affairs, and C.-E Dinesen who became Commander Captain in the Danish Navy.

Every day, Carlo began the day with a small speech to the

newly arrived prisoners: "I am a prisoner just like you. I've been forced to take this job, and it's my duty to keep you in order, so you might as well do it voluntarily. We have no option of doing it differently. So, take it easy."

But behind the scenes, Carlo and his staff were secretly preparing for a possible quick evacuation of the entire camp. A number of wooden benches were constructed with cross boards under the seats. When they were raised up against a fence, they

Carlo's "Guest Book" for the prisoners in Camp 2

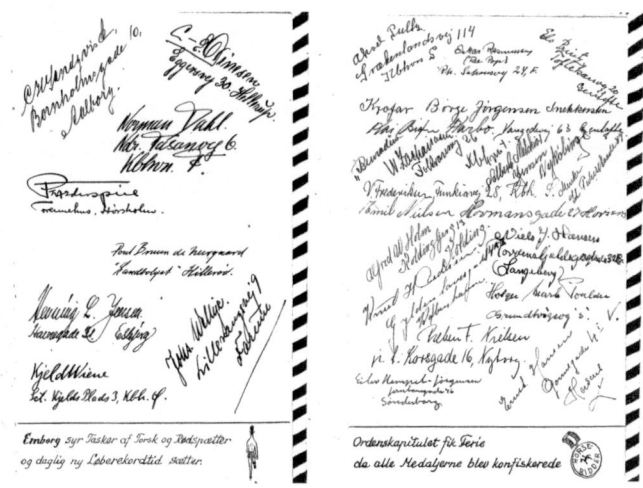

The first two pages (of a total of 42) in Carlo's Guest Book

built a gangway bridge that you could run upon. A lot of work in the camp required the movement of earth masses, but there were no wheelbarrows. So the prisoners built a number of "carry-barrows", which could also function as ladders and were long enough to reach the top of the barbed wire fence surrounding the camp. Carlo had calculated that, in an emergency, the entire camp of 175 men could be evacuated in three minutes. They were never used for this purpose, but on one occasion they could have been used. This was when Sea Captain Poul Ib Gjessing and three other prisoners arrived in Camp 2. Gjessing was in real trouble, since he had been the leader of a large resistance group which had performed sabotages in northern Jutland. The Germans had found a large amount of weapons in his home. During several nights, Carlo tried to convince Gjessing and his three fellow prisoners to escape with the help of the "ladders". Carlo said to him, "Your life is in danger, all your lives are in danger. You are in a hell of a lot of trouble, and sooner or later you are going to be executed." But Gjessing would not be persuaded, and shortly afterwards a covered truck arrived suddenly. Four names were called out. A week later, Wassermann came to Carlo and told him that Gjessing and his three companions had been executed.

In Memorium pages in Carlo's Guest Book for four executed prisoners

61

"German concentration camp" – these words usually evoke horrifying mental images. But that was not the situation in Denmark, at least not in the beginning. The Danish prisoners enjoyed relatively sanitary conditions and the food was adequate in both quantity and content. Only four men occupied each room in the barracks. Some communication with family was permitted, although under strict censorship, but even family visits could occur. Thus it was possible for Elsa and Aage, as well as Elsa's father, to visit Carlo in Horserød concentration camp once during the summer of 1944. Elsa was eight months pregnant, and the three of them walked slowly along the barbed wire to the guard post. At the camp gate, a message was sent to Wassermann, the German commander. Wassermann interrupted his lunch and with a bit of food still in his mouth ran to Carlo's barrack to tell him the good news, that his wife, son and father-in-law had arrived at the camp. At that time, Carlo and Wassermann had actually managed to develop a relatively friendly relationship, even though they were on different sides of the occupation. The reunion of the family took place in a hall, and the joy of seeing each other was overwhelming. Elsa and her father were able to talk with Carlo, while Aage played with a round chair which he had found and actually was more interested in – after the first long hug with Carlo.

Wassermann turned out to be quite indulgent towards Carlo's frequent, obstinate and rather challenging attitudes against the German camp leadership. One such occasion arose when Wassermann made a surprise inspection of one of the barracks. It was forbidden to smoke, but cigarettes had been smuggled into the camp and were available to the inmates. Card-playing was also prohibited, but Carlo's homemade playing cards were popular with his staff. On this occasion, Wassermann, with Carlo in his wake, abruptly threw open the door to the first room.

Some of Carlo's homemade Horserød playing cards

There sat Federspiel, Dignesen, Skipper and Rassow, engulfed in heavy cigarette smoke. The cigarettes were gone, but some playing cards were lying on the table. Skipper stood up but held his hands behind his back. Many years later Carlo described the resulting dialogue (which was actually conducted in German): "Sandqvist, it smells of tobacco smoke in here!", Wassermann yelled. "No, definitely not," Carlo said, "at least, I can't smell anything." "Well, maybe I'm wrong," Wassermann replied, "maybe it doesn't." Then Wassermann turned to Skipper: "What are you hiding behind your back?" "Nothing." "Show me!" And so Skipper showed his hand – "Full House!" Wassermann proceeded to confiscate the playing cards. But as soon as they were outside the room again, Carlo got all his playing cards back – and then Wassermann walked away.

On the war front, the situation was worsening for the Germans. After their defeat in Stalingrad in early 1943, the fortunes of war turned. And on June 6, 1944, the Great Allied invasion took place in Normandy. The Germans became more and more nervous; some began seeing what lay ahead. In Denmark, too, the Germans started to take precautionary action, in case a second invasion would take place on Jutland's west coast. The Danish Cooperation Government resigned as early as August, 1943, and now the Germans were no longer confident that the country would remain calm in case of a crisis. The Germans therefore wanted to move the Danish Horserød prisoners from Zealand to the German border in southern Jutland, so that they could be transferred quickly to Germany, if need be. A new concentration camp was therefore built in Frøslev near the Danish border town of Padborg. As a first step, it was ready to receive approximately 750 Horserød prisoners in August, 1944. One problem for the Germans was that there were already over

1,000 prisoners in the two camps in Horserød. It was therefore decided that some of the prisoners, against whom the Germans had lesser charges, would be interrogated again, and 250 of them subsequently released. Since the Germans had never found any proper evidence against Carlo, he was called to interrogation again and thus got high hopes for release. But Peter Jakob, whose carelessness originally had been the cause of Carlo's internment, was interrogated at the same time as Carlo in an adjoining room. Carlo hung on to his usual lie, but Peter Jakob broke down and revealed the size and scope of Carlo's resistance group. Carlo was now destined for Frøslev.

The plan to relocate the prisoners to the German border was well-known in the Danish resistance movement, and a very bold plan for a rescue attempt had been drawn up. The prisoners were to be shipped from Elsinore with a ferry that was being converted to a prisoner transport ship in Odense. The Danish ferry crew had been infiltrated with resistance men, and some "safe" German crew members had been bribed with large sums of money. It was not uncommon for Germans in Denmark to take bribes, especially in the final stages of the war. The resistance plan was such that, when the ferry with the prisoners had left the harbour in Elsinore and sailed out to the middle of The Sound (Øresund) between Denmark and Sweden, it would be taken over by the resistance men and set full speed eastward, straight towards Hälsingborg in Sweden, instead of turning North. Two Swedish frigates were ready to sail in behind the ferry as soon as it had passed the middle of The Sound to protect it against any German artillery from Kronborg Castle in Elsinore.

In Horserød, only Captain Digmann and his staff in Camp 1 and Carlo and his staff in Camp 2 had been involved in these plans, through secret information channels. Their task was now to keep the other prisoners calm if shooting took place during the final takeover of the ship on The Sound. On the night of Friday, August 11, 1944, a command was issued that the roughly 750 Horserød prisoners should hand in their bedding, pack their belongings and be ready for transport. At dawn on Saturday morning, the prisoners were ordered into Danish buses that transported them to the port of Elsinore. The excitement was at the highest level among Carlo and the few other leaders who were familiar with the plans for the escape. Total shock took over when, instead of the Danish ferry docked at the quay, there was a large German camouflaged troop transport ship, the M/S *Mars,* which was swarming with armed German soldiers. Furthermore, two smaller German naval vessels and a submarine were located between M/S *Mars* and Sweden. What had happened? Where was the Danish ferry? It was actually still in Odense after having been blown up by members of a smaller resistance group. They had known about the plans for transfer of the prisoners from Horserød to Frøslev, but were unaware of the escape plans. The group wanted to prevent the transfer and had therefore blown up the ferry.

On Sunday, August 13, the troop transport ship with the prisoners arrived in Flensburg, south of the German border. The mood among the prisoners dropped sharply when they realised that they now were in Germany: Would it be one of those terrible German concentration camps that was the ultimate goal? But soon they saw a long line of red Danish buses standing behind the quayside buildings. And the ultimate goal was the Frøslev concentration camp after all. Six days later Elsa gave birth to Carlo's third son in Aalborg.

Chapter 7: Escape to Sweden, Autumn 1944

Sunday, August 13, 1944

The concentration camp in Frøslev was not fully completed when the Horserød prisoners arrived on August 13, 1944, as the first inhabitants. But the development of the camp was rapid since the Germans emptied many of their prisons in Denmark and sent prisoners to Frøslev. Soon the number of prisoners was up in 1,500 and eventually it would be over 2,000. Captain Digmann, who had been the Danish leader of Camp 1 in Horserød, now became the Danish leader of the entire Frøslev camp. Carlo became the camp supervisor with the task of organizing and distributing work to the 1,500 prisoners daily. The Germans installed a platoon of about twenty SS men which guarded the camp. For the daily contact with the prisoners there were many German "Wachtmeistere", soldiers from the German Wehrmacht. Wassermann from Horserød was commissioned to be the German Hauptwachtmeister, in command of the other Wachtmeistere.

Frøslev concentration camp (in 1964)

*Hauptwachtmeister Wassermann in Frøslev, and
"Advertisement" designed by a Frøslev prisoner
(Photos: Danish Freedom Museum)*

Frøslev now carried on the tradition from Horserød to be a relatively "soft" concentration camp with acceptable conditions for the prisoners. But the Germans broke their promise to the Danes not to send certain prisoners to German concentration camps, and after a month more than 200 prisoners had been sent to Germany[1]. Although the prisoners were unaware of the full extent of these camps, they were known to be dreadful. The threat of being sent to Germany weighed heavily on the every-

---

1 At the end of September, close to 300 Danish policemen were sent to German concentration camps. Among them was Carlo's brother, Børge. He was sent to Buchenwald where he remained until the end of December, 1944, when he was transferred to the Neuengammen concentration camp. Late in April, 1945, he came to Sweden with Folke Bernadotte's "White Buses" of liberation. His health got a severe blow in Buchenwald. He never got over his nightmares, which would often frighten his family at night.

day life of the Frøslev prisoners.

Each morning, the 1,500 prisoners lined up in four rows on the camp main square with the German officers and NCOs standing next to them. Captain Digmann was also present. In front of the rows stood Carlo with the day's list of jobs that the Germans wanted to be done. It could be anything from kitchen duty, carpentry and house building to ditch digging and tree-felling in the woods outside the camp. It could take some time to assign the different work teams, but Carlo had developed a useful system that worked smoothly.

One day in September, after the distribution of labour was completed, Carlo had returned to his barrack and in his room stood his comrade Federspiel, waiting with the words: "Your wife is standing outside". "WHAT?!", Carlo exclaimed. "Yes, your wife is outside the camp." Carlo rushed off to the front gate through the various fences which he, as supervisor, could pass through without problems. The German guards, incre-dibly, even saluted him as he passed their posts. But when he arrived at the front gate, it was too late. Elsa was gone.

A few days earlier, Elsa had arrived in Padborg in a vain attempt to obtain a meeting with Carlo in the Frøslev camp. She had taken along two small photos which she planned to give to Carlo, one of Carlo's newborn son whom he had not yet seen. In addition, she had two milk bottles filled with Scandinavian vodka, camouflaged as strawberry juice, as well as sausage and a package of butter.

The Frøslev camp was only a few kilometres outside Pad-borg, so Elsa walked to the camp carrying her presents. But when she came near the outer barbed wire fence, she was stop-ped by a guard in one of the watchtowers. "Hundertfünfzig meter zurück!", he screamed threateningly several times. That guard, originally from the Horserød camp, had the reputation of being "a real asshole". Elsa shouted back to the guard that she wanted to come in and meet Carlo. "Hundertfünfzig meter zurück!" was the answer that came back again. Elsa retreated the commanded 150 metres and stayed there all day in the cold before she finally walked back to Padborg in the evening.

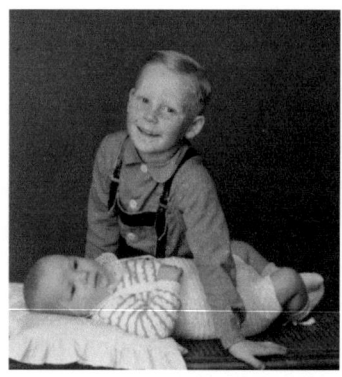

The two small photos which Elsa wanted to give to Carlo –
left: Aage with his new little brother, right: Elsa and Aage

The German guards were not always to be played with. One day, a prisoner in the camp had come too close to the barbed wire fence. There were many light poles placed in an imaginary line a few metres from the fence. It formed a forbidden zone running along the inside of the fence. The prisoner had been walking, preoccupied in his own thoughts, and had accidentally crossed the imaginary boundary. A guard in the watchtower shot him in the head with two shots – he died.

In Padborg that evening, Elsa met a Mrs. Skjoldager, who had somehow obtained a passport to the camp to meet her husband. She had promised to tell her husband that Elsa would be outside the camp, but nothing happened on the following days, apart from new "Hundertfünfzig-meter-zurück!" commands, issued by the same guard. After three days of waiting outside the Frøslev camp, Elsa gave up and went back to Aalborg. This guard would return in other contexts, and Carlo and Elsa always called him Hundertfünfzig-meter-zurück after that.

The major military transport line between Germany and Norway was the railway up through the whole of Jutland from Padborg to Fredrikshavn, where German troops and military equipment were loaded onto ships for further voyage to Oslo. In the autumn of 1944, the Danish resistance groups sharply increased their sabotage against these transports. The German countermove was to place ten Danish prisoners on the trains as hostages in a cattle car just behind the locomotives. These prisoners would be selected in the Frøslev camp at the breakfast meal and then immediately transported to be put on the trains in Padborg. The Germans sadistically referred to these Danish hostages as "Himmelfarhtskommandon" (Ascension Squads).

Carlo was selected as hostage number eleven, which meant number one in the second hostage team. That he was now on a list as number eleven out of fifteen hundred prisoners in Frøslev, was due to Peter Jakob's disclosure of the real extent of Carlo's resistance activities in Aalborg at the last interrogation in Horserød. With the help of another prisoner, who worked in the administration office of the Frøslev camp, Carlo had discovered that his file stated that he was a dangerous saboteur and terrorist. Carlo had immediately understood that if he were to survive the hostage trip up through Jutland and back again, he would almost certainly be transported subsequently to a German concentration camp. If the train was sabotaged on the way and the hostages survived, they would immediately be shot afterwards. Back in his barrack, Carlo said to Federspiel, Emborg and Dinesen (his senior staff from Horserød): "So, now I feel that my life is in danger". The four had earlier agreed that if anyone felt that his life was in danger, he should try to escape. "If I get the chance, then I flee! Then you'll not see me again." Everyone approved the plan. It was important that his friends gave their approval because the Germans regularly punished the remaining prisoners if someone fled. Emborg now gave Carlo his knitted Icelandic sweater, Dinesen gave him his ration cards and Federspiel gave him money. And so they wished Carlo "Good Luck!". Together with his nine fellow hostages, Carlo was transported by truck to Padborg. There they were loaded onto the cattle car behind the locomotive on a very long freight train, which carried tanks and other motorized vehicles, as well as a large contingent of German soldiers. There were no benches in the cattle car, but plenty of straw on the floor. There was a small compartment at one end of the car where four German guards from the Frøslev camp were located; one of them was Hundertfünfzig-meter-zurück.

Tuesday, October 10, 1944.

After a long journey up through Jutland and a stationary overnight stay at the station in Randers, the German transport train arrived at Aalborg Central Station on Tuesday morning, October 10, 1944. Carlo had secretly raised the idea of a combined escape with three of his fellow hostages whom he trusted. He had previously met one of them at Aalborg Airport, the other two he knew from Frøslev. But none of them wanted to attempt an escape, so Carlo had to rely on himself in his planning. The train stopped at the station and the door of the cattle car rolled open, it had not been locked. Carlo sat down on the floor, on the bottom step. Then a Danish railway worker came sneaking past the open door and whispered, "Is there anything I can do for you?" He continued to walk past the wagon, but came back shortly after that. Carlo whispered to him: "Look, you can go to Bornholmsgade no. 10. I'm Lieutenant Sandqvist. Tell my wife that she should go underground together with our two children". "OK", and then the railway worker disappeared from the platform.

About an hour later, Carlo, standing in the cattle car door-way, suddenly saw a familiar figure running along the platform towards him with a small bundle in her arms. It was Elsa car-rying the now two-month-old son whom Carlo still had not seen. Hundertfünfzig-meter-zurück, who was standing on the platform in front of the car, saw her as well. He asked Carlo if he knew this lady. "I sure do! That's my wife. And I want to come down and talk to her for a bit." The guard initially refused, but eventually gave in. Carlo jumped down from the cattle care, and warmly embraced Elsa. And now, for the first time, he held his third son in his arms. Carlo now conveyed to Elsa in a low-key manner that he intended to escape. She then wanted to get him a pistol. But he would have none of that; there should be no shooting in connection with the escape. And now it was time for her and the kids to go underground. All too soon the visit was over and Carlo had to climb up in the cattle car again. Elsa slowly walked back along the platform with the baby in her arms. After a while, the train started, crossed the Limfjord and continued north.

In Brønderslev, 25 km north of Aalborg, the cattle car was decoupled from the train and placed on a side track while the rest of the train continued to another station for unloading. Both doors in the cattle car were opened fully. Three of the German guards went out to refresh themselves in a nearby restaurant, while the fourth stood guard in front of the car stretching his legs. The hostages remained inside the car. Suddenly, one of the prisoners in the hostage emerged from the German guards' compartment with a loaded machine gun in his hands: "Look what I found in there. And there is one more in there". Carlo jumped up, a better opportunity for escape would never materialize. But none of the others wanted, or dared, to take advantage of the situation, and Carlo was forced to return to his original plan.

The long train came back, now empty, and the cattle car was coupled to the locomotive again. Carlo had decided to jump off the train in Aalborg because he knew that city well, and that was where he had all his connections with the resistance movement. In Aalborg, there was a railway curve close to the city hospital, where the train would slow down to a speed of under ten kilometres per hour. Directly after the bend, there was a spot where the corner of the hospital was almost touching the railway. At this point, Carlo planned to jump.

The railway curve in Aalborg where Carlo jumped off the moving train, and the hospital behind which he took shelter

Carlo had been standing by the door, which was still unlocked and slightly opened so he could peek out and see where he was. By the other door stood the fellow prisoner with whom Carlo had earlier entrusted his escape plans – very pale because he knew what was about to take place. The train finally slowed down, and at precisely the right time Carlo threw open the door. "Oh, I'm getting so sick, I have to throw up", he gasped – an excuse he had made up in case he would get caught. He hopped down onto the bottom step of the car and then jumped off the train. Hundertfünfzig-meter-zurück sat about five metres from the door and fiddled with something, and the other three guards were in their compartment. Hundert-fünfzig-meter-zurück screamed like a wounded animal when he saw Carlo disappear through the door. A couple of somersaults later, followed by a high jump over a fence, and Carlo was behind the corner of the hospital building. Just before he disappeared behind the corner, he glanced back at the disappearing train. There stood Hundertfünfzig-meter-zurück with one foot on the second step on the car and his machine gun pointing at Carlo. He had hurried into the guard compartment to retrieve his weapon and then crept out onto the step as the train continued on its journey.

At the same time, Elsa was standing on Aalborg Central Station waiting for the train with Carlo to arrive. She had a pistol, wrapped in a paper bag, hidden in the sleeve of her coat. Despite Carlo's wishes, she had procured a loaded pistol, which she wanted to give to Carlo before his attempted escape. At last the train slowly entered the station and came to a full stop. Elsa scampered across the tracks to the platform by the cattle car, attempting to get in touch with Carlo. German soldiers now came running, and there was great confusion. Elsa overheard how they discussed with each other that Carlo had just jumped off the train and that he had probably been shot. Hundert-fünfzig-meter-zurück was also there – and he now recognized Elsa. She was arrested on the spot. The loaded pistol was still hidden in her coat sleeve. If it were discovered, the consequences would be severe – possession of weapons resulted in the death penalty.

Immediately after his escape, Carlo ran as fast as he could past the hospital with blood dripping from his hands, which had been injured while he was rolling over on the railway stone shards beside the moving train. After thoroughly frightening a lady that he ran past, he forced himself to slow down to a leisurely pace and hid his bleeding hands in his pockets. With his heart pounding, he finally reached the apartment of one of Aalborg's leading resistance fighters, Simonsen. A meeting with other freedom fighters was taking place there. Great was the surprise and joy when Carlo entered the apartment, a free man for the first time in six months. Carlo immediately received first aid from Simonsen's mother, who was also there. Suddenly, the telephone interrupted the freedom fighters' happy discussion about the successful escape.

The phone call came from an observer from the resistance movement, who had been at the railway station, awaiting the German transport train's arrival in Aalborg: "Mrs. Sandqvist has been arrested. By the Gestapo!" As though struck by lightning, everyone fled out of the apartment in a great rush, because Elsa knew where Carlo probably would hide after the escape. The emotional strain finally became too much for Carlo, and out on the street, he collapsed and became utterly hysterical. Only a mighty slap in the face got him back in balance. The resistance fighters now all dispersed in different directions, and Carlo was taken to another safe apartment.

Meanwhile, Elsa was taken out of the train station and brutally pushed into the back seat of an Opel for the short drive to the High School Home, the Gestapo headquarters. Next to her sat a short fat Gestapo man, and two other persons were in the front seats. Elsa feverishly thought that she had to get rid of the pistol. Finally, she put her hand on the Gestapo man's thigh and said: "You can't allow this to happen. I have a small child at home". Slowly, her hand slid down between his legs, and then she squeezed gently and "lovingly" on his penis and testicles. While he sat there concentrating on what her hand was doing, Elsa relieved herself of the paper bag containing the pistol with the other hand and gently pushed it down into the gap between the seat and the backrest of the car. When they arrived at the High School Home and got out of the car, Elsa turned around to retrieve her gloves and cigarettes. To her great dismay, she discerned that part of the bag was sticking out of the seat gap. She decidedly left both the gloves and the cigarettes on the seat.

Inside the High School Home, Elsa was ushered into an office where an SS man in uniform sat with his boots slung onto a large desk and a horse whip in one hand. He began to question her. The SS man blamed Elsa for Carlo's escape from the train. It was she who had gone to Frøslev to tempt him. Now she would be going to Frøslev instead of Carlo. Right in the middle of the interrogation, the Gestapo commander in Aalborg suddenly walked past the office and looked inside. When he saw Elsa sitting there, he became pale in the face and stopped for a brief moment. Then he walked on. A short time later the phone rang and the SS man answered. It was the Gestapo commander: "Mrs. Sandqvist must be released. Now! She must be be set free." The SS man scolded Elsa thoroughly,

77

but released her.

Why? That question puzzled both Carlo and Elsa for many years afterwards. The only thing that could possibly explain the release was that Elsa knew the Gestapo commander's Danish mistress and had shown her kindness on several occasions. A small example of this was once when Elsa and Aage were at Konditori Kristine, Aalborg's finest confectionery, which was always crowded. Aage was halfway through a slice of layer cake when the Gestapo commander came in accompanied by his mistress. There were no chairs free except for a few at Elsa's table, and the Gestapo commander asked if they could sit there. Yes, they could, but the situation was highly embarrassing, because everyone knew that Gestapo had interned Elsa's husband and Aage's father in the Frøslev concentration camp. They sat down at Elsa's table and engaged in small talk. Finally, Elsa said, "Aage, hurry up and finish that cake. We have to go now."

Anyway, Elsa quickly called Simonsen after her release and said she had been set free. Simonsen did not believe her and asked her to walk along the street where he lived. She did so, and he came biking towards her. They talked for a while, and Simonsen finally concluded with a little gallows humour: "I think that you should go back and pick up your gloves and cigarettes."

Carlo did not spend a long time in the secure apartment but was moved to a villa cellar in Vejgaard, a suburb of Aalborg. The owner of the villa was Dr. Warberg, a medical doctor who hid refugees in his basement on various occasions. As Carlo sat down in the cellar, Dr. Warberg was examining some young athletes in his office. One of them was the brother of Elsa's girl-friend, Inger. The young people were talking about Lieutenant Sandqvist having jumped off a moving train and escaped from the Germans – that was very exciting, but it was a pity that his wife had been caught instead. "Oh no," said Inger's brother, "she was actually released! She is free again." Warberg jumped up and ran down into the basement, with his stethoscope flapping around his neck, to tell Carlo the good news. And Carlo immediately understood where Elsa would subsequently be found.

Aage was already in good care with his Grandma and Grandpa in Gug. After her release, Elsa had hurried to her close friends, Helga and Knud Hansen, who lived on Langelandsgade. With her, she had the baby who still had no name. The little boy would be handed over to Knud and Helga, who would take care of him in the uncertain future. A few days later, a freedom fighter came to this address. He picked up Elsa and brought her to a very emotional reunion with Carlo in Dr. Warberg's basement. After the Germans had found Elsa's pistol in the back seat of the Opel, she was once again hunted game, just like Carlo. The resistance movement in Aalborg now found it too dangerous to have Carlo and Elsa remain in Aalborg, and anywhere else in Denmark. Development of plans to send them to Sweden was now of high priority. Meanwhile, they sat waiting for ten days, cooling their heels in Dr. Warberg's basement.

The Germans had initiated a big campaign in Aalborg to find Carlo. One German, who did not participate in this hunt, was Hundertfünfzig-meter-zurück. It was only discovered a year and a half after the end of the war when one day Carlo received a letter from him in Germany. In the letter, Hundertfünfzig-meter-zurück wrote that he had been greatly moved by Carlo's first meeting with his newborn son and wife on the platform in Aalborg Central Station. He, himself, had a wife and five children in Germany whom he had not seen in a very long time. That he, as the main hostage guard, had not stopped Carlo from escaping led to his internment for three months in a German concentration camp. Hundertfünfzig-meter-zurück had 'changed places with Carlo'.

The resistance movement now produced false identification papers for Carlo and Elsa. They got "employment" as engine apprentice and kitchen help on a schooner located in Aalborg harbour. The regular ship's crew consisted of five people, now expanded to seven. After ten days of delay due to the presence of English mines in the Limfjord outlet to Kattegatt at Hals and subsequent mine sweeping, the day of departure finally arrived.

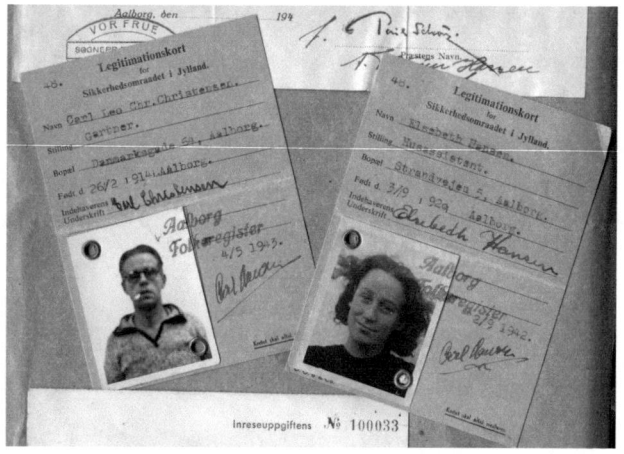

Carlo and Elsa's false identification papers

Two German soldiers inspected the ship before departure according to the regulations. They glanced lazily down on Carlo through the machine room valve. He had sprayed oil on himself and was walking around down there with an oil can. Elsa stood in the ship's kitchen and was cleaning fish. The

Germans approved all the papers, and, with a friendly pat on Elsa's bottom, they wished her "Happy journey, Sister!"

The schooner finally left Aalborg and eventually reached the Kattegatt. There were plenty of waves here, and Elsa got really seasick. Carlo, on the other hand, went up on deck and enjoyed the fresh night air as well as the promise of the forthcoming freedom that Sweden would now offer[2]. But as Carlo was now looking at the sea and the sky, he couldn't help but think of the two sons they had left behind in the German-occupied Aalborg. Aage would once again be without his parents for a longer period, even though he had his Grandma and Grandpa. How would the youngest son connect with Knud and Helga, and what would happen to that relationship when Carlo and Elsa returned to Denmark sometime in the future? The schooner sailed very slowly by engine across the Kattegatt, and it took thirty hours before they were in total safety in the port of Gothenburg. Once on Swedish soil, Carlo and Elsa were welcomed to Sweden by a Swedish policeman with the words: "Well, have you also blown up Forum[3]?"

[2] The Germans continued to place hostages on the transport trains for a few more months, but now under increased surveillance, and the hostages were chained together in twos. In the end, they tired because the resistance movement came up with solutions for sabotage where hostages were not threatened. Of the 210 prisoners placed as hostages by the Germans on the "Himmelfartskommandon" tours, Carlo was the only one who managed to escape.

[3] Forum was a large famous building in Copenhagen which the resistance movement destroyed in a spectacular action. Claiming participation in that campaign was not uncommon when Danish refugees sought asylum in Sweden.

PART 2: Sweden 1944 - 1945

Chapter 8: Danish Refugee in Sweden, 1944

Carlo's first action in Gothenburg was to get rid of the oil-soaked clothes, buy a new suit, and then present himself at the Refugee Office. He was welcomed there by a Danish military pilot, Captain H. P. Michael Hansen, who also was a refugee, since the autumn of 1943. He had handled issues concerning Danish refugees arriving in Gothenburg since February, 1944.

In the autumn of 1943, the Germans had carried out the large operation, "Safari", in Denmark, during which also some Danish pilot officers were interned, while some managed to flee to Sweden. The so-called "cooperation policy" between Denmark and Germany, which had been introduced after the German occupation of Denmark, became more and more unsustainable as time went on. In August, 1943, the situation collapsed totally after nationwide strikes, demonstrations and uprisings. The Danish cooperation government resigned on August 29. The Germans seized the opportunity and immediately started the Safari operation. They attacked the remaining Danish military installations on Zealand and Funen, where some regular war activities took place in the form of sharp shootings from both sides – 23 Danish soldiers died, and 40 were wounded. The Germans then disarmed and interned 4,600 Danish officers and soldiers. However, some of them managed to flee across the Sound to Sweden, where they would eventually form the core of the "Danish Brigade" in Sweden.

The few pilots, who came to Sweden at that time, had high hopes of finding a transport to Britain and then join the Allied

Air Force in its fight against the Germans. That was also true of Carlo. But Britain had enough pilots at that time and was not particularly interested in getting some Danes into its Royal Air Force. Also, transporting people from Sweden to the British Isles was very difficult. There were a few unarmed Swedish Mosquito bombers, which occasionally made the trip from Bromma to Scotland, but these were reserved for more important persons. For example, the Danish physicist and Nobel laureate, Niels Bohr, endured such a journey in early October, 1943, bundled up against the cold and hidden in the plane's bomb deck. Niels Bohr had fled from Denmark the week before, during the big action against Danish Jews, initiated by the Germans. Therefore, there were no available immediate transports of Danish pilots to England. Carlo and Elsa were forced to accept the idea of a new existence in Sweden.

Carlo's emergency visa, Elsa also got the same

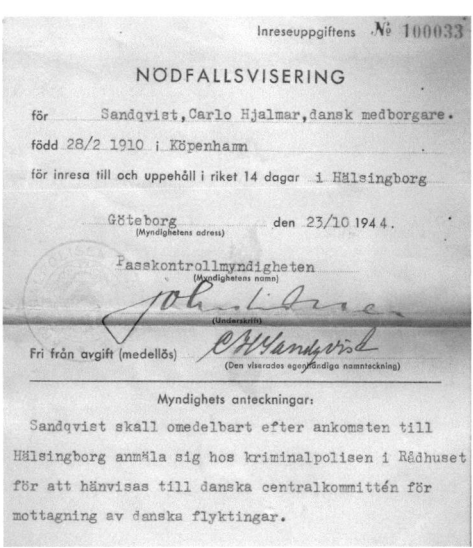

The Swedish passport control authority quickly issued emergency visas to Carlo and Elsa and ordered them to travel to

Hälsingborg immediately. There they should present themselves to the police in the town hall, who would, in turn, refer them to the Danish Central Committee for the Reception of Danish Refugees. Before leaving Gothenburg, Carlo revisited the Refugee Office to discuss his future with Captain Hansen. Carlo was deeply disappointed by not being allowed to travel to England and continue his fight against the Germans in the Royal Air Force. He had no great desire to sit in a refugee camp anywhere in Sweden and passively await the development of the course of the war. After already spending half a year in the German concentration camps in Horserød and Frøslev, he was fed up with camp life and did not want to continue such an existence, although it would be different in Sweden. Captain Hansen did his best to try to calm Carlo. He informed him that there was a Danish military refugee organization in Sweden, which in strictest secrecy, but with the approval of neutral Sweden, was preparing for a return to Denmark.

The organization was camouflaged as a camp to train a police force that would help maintain order in Denmark following a possible German retreat from that country. After a while, this police force grew into the Danish Brigade in Sweden. This Brigade also included about ten Danish pilots, who had already been secretly stationed on various airbases in Sweden.

Captain Hansen promised to do his best to get Carlo placed on such an airbase quickly. But until then, Carlo would have to be so kind as to orderly submit to Swedish refugee policies.

Therefore, Carlo and Elsa took the next train to Hälsingborg in southern Sweden, where they were initially taken care of by the regional reception center for Danish refugees. Residence visas, which were issued by the Swedish Social Board, were valid for all of Sweden, except for protected military areas where special permits were required. They were now recommended to go to the area around Tingsryd in Småland, which was near "Sofielund", a camp that housed the growing "Danish Police Force". The Danish Commission in Stockholm would support them financially until they found suitable jobs. They were also awarded Swedish ration cards.

Carlo and Elsa's
Swedish ration cards

Carlo and Elsa's environment during
their first period in Sweden

It was not easy for Carlo and Elsa to find work in the Tingsryds area, and Carlo became more and more anxious that Captain Hansen should fulfill his promise to have Carlo placed on an airbase. Meanwhile, Carlo and Elsa enjoyed the excellent environment and the fine cohesion of Danish refugees in the area, a necessary therapy after the formidable hardships that they had endured in the last six months in Denmark. Now they got in touch with other Danes who would eventually become close friends. One such person was Pedro Gauguin. His surname is unique and clearly brings to mind the famous French painter of the late nineteenth century, Paul Gauguin. Pedro was actually Paul Gauguin's grandson. Paul Gauguin had been married to a Danish woman, Mette, whom he abandoned when he traveled to Tahiti to continue his artistic life. Mette stayed in Denmark with their five children; the oldest son, Emile, was Pedro's father. Pedro had been in Sweden for a month when he befriended Carlo and Elsa. He had been a police officer in Denmark but managed to escape to Sweden when the Germans carried out their round-up of the Danish police in mid-September – the same event that forced Carlo's brother, Børge, to Buchenwald. Pedro continued his work as a police officer in Denmark after the war, but also pursued his artistic painting career. Carlo and Elsa eventually had half a dozen of Pedro's works hanging in their future homes after the war. Having a Gauguin hanging on the wall was not all that bad, even though the artist was Pedro and not Paul.

In the autumn of 1944, Sweden had a developed a reasonably large refugee problem. There had been only about 500 Danish refugees in Sweden the year before. However, after the collapse of the Danish cooperation government in the autumn of 1943, and the resulting German Safari action against the Danish military and their unsuccessful round-up of the Jews in Denmark, there were 7,000 Danish refugees in Sweden. By the end of the year, that number had increased to 10,500. One year later, in 1944, the figure was 14,800, and at the end of the war, it was 18,000. The corresponding development for Norwegian refugees was from 17,000 at the end of 1943 to 43,000 at the end of the war. To these numbers should be added the 80,000

Finnish children, who had been moved to Sweden for "safe-keeping". And there were also many refugees from the Baltic States. Sweden really stood up for its neighbours during the second half of the war.

Pedro Gauguin creates one of his paintings at Carlo and Elsa's summer cottage in Blokhus on the northwest coast of Jutland, in the 1940s after the war

Chapter 9: The Danish Brigade in Sweden and its Air Unit, 1944

Sweden's neutrality policy in 1943 made all forms of military aid to Denmark impossible. The Germans carefully monitored everything that Sweden did. The big question was therefore what the Swedes would do with the growing number of Danish refugees, most of whom really wanted to return to Denmark to fight the German occupation power. The problem was not new to Sweden, since it had already been forced to deal with a large number of Norwegian refugees, who had similar desires, namely to get rid of the Germans in Norway. After careful consideration of the matter at the government level in October and November, a council decision was reached on December 3, 1943. This decision was to establish a Danish "police camp" in Sofielund in southern Småland, a camp similar to the Norwegian police camps already existing in other parts of Sweden. Here would be housed 500 Danish refugees who would receive police training from the Swedish police. The training would prepare the Danes for a return to Denmark after some future German withdrawal. Since the Germans had confiscated all weapons in Denmark, general order could be in danger of collapsing during a transitional period. There existed a serious concern that the communists, and probably other illegal groups, would take up arms in the event of a German collapse. A Danish police force in Sofielund could therefore be deployed to Denmark and would guarantee the maintenance of law and order. But under no circumstance should the training in the police camp appear to be military training. With such a procedure, Sweden would still appear to be neutral and not have to intervene in a neighbouring country in the event of a

German collapse. Sweden could thus continue staying out of the war.

The Danish Brigade's camp in Sofielund

The Swedish and Danish flags in the camp of the Danish Brigade in Sofielund (Photos: National Museum, Denmark)

Although the Germans themselves did not think that they would be forced to leave Denmark in the future, they could just barely accept that Sweden implemented the plan for this camp – communists were not popular among the Germans either. However, only police weapons should be used in Sofielund, at least initially.

It was recognized early on that the establishment of a police camp required a central board for leadership. Several Danish police camps would eventually be established in Sweden, including one in Ryds Brunn. This camp was dedicated to *real* police officers who fled Denmark in September, 1944, when the Germans abolished the Danish police system and arrested the members of the police force. It was in connection with that action that Carlo's brother, Børge, was captured and sent to Buchenwald. And it was in connection with that campaign that Pedro Gauguin had fled to Sweden and shortly thereafter had begun his long-standing friendship with Carlo and Elsa, in the region around Ryds Brunn.

In Denmark, following the Safari campaign at the end of August, 1943, there no longer existed any official government, that is, no government agency which could exercise constitutional power. All power was now in the hands of the Germans with Dr. Werner Best as the German leader, the "Reichsbevollmächtiger". However, the Danish political parties continued their activities in a kind of shadow government, with the former prime minister, Vilhelm Buhl, as the Danish leader. In the end of October, the Germans revoked the internment of the Danish officers and other military personnel after receiving a promise that the Danish military would not carry out hostile action against the Germans in Denmark. Vilhelm Buhl soon realized that the growing police force in Sweden could be a way of "employing" a large part of the liberated military personnel in a meaningful way. Many had fled to Sweden. However, they would need a firm hand to guide them in the new country. Therefore, after consultation with the Danish Commander-in-Chief, General Ebbe Gärtz, Buhl sent Major General Kristian Knudtzon, and a smaller staff of seven members, to Sweden in early November. They would exert the required leadership. A credit of 5 million Swedish Crowns was provisionally made available to the new "Danish Refugee Office" by the Swedish State Bank with the promise that Denmark's National Bank would repay the loan after the war. The Danish Brigade in Sweden was established, and the "Command for Military Refugees", with Knudtzon as its head, was stationed in Stockholm. By January, 1945, the staff had grown to 30 people, and in May, 1945, the Brigade itself comprised a force of 5,000 men, divided into five battalions with full armaments.

A handful of Danish pilots had also fled to Sweden in 1943 and 1944, and the Brigade's staff was investigating the possibility of establishing a tactical flight support for the operation. The commander of the Swedish Air Force, Major General Bengt Nordenskjöld, had some difficulty seeing tactical flight support as a police matter and expressed concern about the idea at his first meeting with Knudtzon in February, 1944. But after a consultation with the Swedish government, Nordenskjöld returned a month later with a decision to place ten Danish pilots on five Swedish airbases, two pilots on each base. The five airbases were F3 (Malmslätt), F4 (Östersund), F8 (Barkarby), F11 (Nyköping), and F12 (Kalmar). The pilots were permitted to undertake flight training, but under no circumstances were they allowed to fly the aircraft themselves – and only accompany as passengers. Civilian attire, or in some exceptional cases

Swedish uniforms without insignia, was the rule, this to avoid attracting unwanted German attention. This strict neutrality requirement worked well and kept the secret activity away from the public eye until September, 1944. In the middle of that month, a B3 bomber (Junkers Ju-86) crashed in central Sweden and the Danish "accompanying passenger", Marine Lieutenant Jørgen Lauritsen, was killed. However, the full extent of the Danish pilots' activities in Sweden remained hidden from the public and could continue without German objections. It could even be expanded as time went on.

The Danish pilots were permitted to fly only as a passenger, which was rather hard on them. As time went on, their numbers slowly grew, and a small number of air technical and ground personnel also arrived and needed employment. Following the Allied invasion of Normandy, on D-Day, June 6, 1944, Sweden increased the number of airbases available to the Danish Brigade to include F6 (Karlsborg) and F9 (Säve) as well. But it was still only "passenger flight" that was permitted. In September of that year, rumours began to flourish that a second Allied invasion was imminent, this time in Denmark on Jutland's west coast, which prompted the Germans to undertake a number of comprehensive defensive activities in Jutland. At the same time, Knudtzon used this so-called "September crisis" to try to convince the Swedes that greater efforts in support of the Danish Brigade were now necessary. He requested a division of eight fighter planes of type J9 (Seversky Republic EP-1) and a bomber division consisting of twelve B17 dive-bombers, manned by voluntary Swedish crews. This request was denied. However, after the September crisis had subsided, the Chief of the Swedish Air Staff, Axel Ljungdal, finally agreed to include six bombers of type B5 (Northrop A-1) and four fighters of type

J8 (Gloster-Gladiator) at the disposal of the Danish Brigade. At the same time, the training of Danish pilots on F4 Östersund, F6 Karlsborg and F12 Kalmar was intensified. More importantly, the Danish pilots were now allowed to fly the aircraft themselves for one hour a month with a Swedish pilot as a passenger. However, the Swedish pride and joy, the new Swedish-produced dive-bomber, B17, remained out of reach for the Danes.

This was the situation as Carlo waited and cooled his heels in the Tingsryd area in mid-November. But then suddenly one day, the long-awaited message came from Captain Hansen at the Refugee Office: In a secret document (Air Force H436c), sent to the Head of the F6 Karlsborg airbase, signed "By Order" by the Swedish Chief of Air Staff, Axel Ljungdahl, on November 14, 1944, it is stated:

On F 6, from 20/11 the following Danish officers will serve:
Lieutenant D. C. Knudsen, Lieutenant E. Möller,
and Lieutenant C. H. Sandqvist.
For their service on airbase, apply the by CFV [Chief of Air Force] *previously issued "Special provisions for Danish officers during their stay at airbase" with the following additions:*
1) Flight activity is completed in the same way as AFT on aircraft B5.
2) Maximum flight time = 3 hours / month.
3) The flights will be planned so that they do not pass over important defence places or areas prohibited to civil aviation.
4) Flights may be extended up to 4 km radius from the airfield.
5) Swedish personnel should always accompany the aircraft.

All that now remained for Carlo was to pack the suitcases as soon as possible and together with Elsa travel to Karlsborg!

Chapter 10: Danish Pilots on Swedish Airbases, 1944 - 1945

The airbase F6 in Karlsborg was a relative newcomer to the Danish Brigade. It had become available to Danish pilots on June 14, 1944. The head of the fighter division and the security service of the Danish Army Air Troops, Lieutenant Colonel H. L. V. Bjarkov, was placed at F6, after spending three months at F8 Barkarby. Bjarkov had come to Sweden as early as October, 1943, as one of the first Danish pilots to escape to Sweden. He had begun in Stockholm, where he worked hard to get Danish pilots placed on Swedish airbases. Bjarkov would eventually become one of only two Danish pilots who managed to get to England. That happened on November 7, 1944, when he was transported to Scotland in a Douglas transport aircraft. In England, he became part of "The Danish Military Mission to SHAEF (Supreme Headquarters Allied Expeditionary Forces)" at General Eisenhower's headquarters. The second Danish pilot to arrive at F6 Karlsborg, on June 14, was Lieutenant Captain E. B. Meincke. He had also initially been at F8 Barkarby. Meincke would eventually become group leader for the Danes at F6, after having spent some time at F9 Säve, outside Gothenburg.

It was really a sort of "musical chairs" between the various airbases for the Danish pilots. When Carlo and Lieutenants Knudsen and Møller arrived at F6 Karlsborg, Bjarkov, Meincke and Lieutenant Captain V. Holm left this airbase to move to other airbases. Holm had fled from Denmark already in the autumn of 1943, just like Bjarkov, and had begun his career in the Danish Brigade's Air Unit on April 14, 1944, at F3 Malmslätt as one of the first ten deployed Danish pilots. Since the

Danes initially were not allowed to fly the aeroplanes themselves, they had to amuse themselves in other ways when not training. Holm has described an interesting exercise that was initiated by an order from the airbase commander at F3 Malmslätt, Colonel Beckhammar. It is reproduced here in Holm's own words, in an English translation:

During the war, many American and British aircraft landed in Sweden. There were also some German planes that landed there and among them a Fokker CV from the Danish airbase Randstaterne.

All units had fixed procedures for handling the arrival of foreign aircraft. Shortly after we arrived in Malmslätt, Beckhammar came up with the idea that I and Danielsen [another Danish pilot] *should participate in an exercise to test the reception procedure, as well as the reaction of the guards, in connection with the arrival a foreign aircraft.*

At the Test & Evaluation Centre, on the other side of the airfield, a Swedish S14 Storch was "changed" to a Luftwaffe aeroplane. Danielsen was dressed up as a saboteur and equipped with a pistol. The pilot was a civilian who was unknown to the airbase personnel, and I was dressed up as a diplomat and provided with a diplomatic passport. We planned to depart from the Test & Evaluation Centre at low altitude – unnoticed by the airbase personnel – and then return to the airfield at 200 - 300 meters altitude.

The day before, the airbase commander had ordered that all ammunition from the guards, as well as from the air defence unit, be handed in for inspection, so that there could be no shooting with danger to the persons involved.

We took off unnoticed and left the airfield at very low

altitude. Then we turned back and climbed to a few hundred metres and approached Malmslätt. On the airfield below, all kinds of activities began, both in the air surveillance towers and on the ground, where technicians had been working on parked aircraft.

The Swedish Fieseler Storch aircraft with German designations (Photo J. B. Danielsen)

We circled the field and went in for landing. Even before our aeroplane came to a full stop, the first guards were around us with their machine guns on the ready. Danielsen quickly jumped out of the plane, but he was overpowered, and the pistol wrenched out of his hand. An attempt on his part to set fire to the aeroplane, with gasoline in a bottle with a rag, was also prevented.

The three of us were then strictly ordered up to the airbase commander's office. We acted and spoke very low-key – in German – but I made them aware that I had diplomatic status and wanted to be treated accordingly.

The "foreign" aircraft has just landed and the crew is arrested. In the background, Danielsen is seen holding a pistol in his hand (Photo J. B. Danielsen)

We had the machine guns aimed at us the whole time, but, knowing that they were not loaded, we took it easy and thought it was all fascinating.

In the office, I began by showing my diplomatic passport and again demanded to be treated according to current laws. Right during the discussion, Danielsen got the impulse to jump out of an open window to keep the guards alert. A technician, who was guarding us with his machine gun, raised his weapon and shot at Danielsen, as he was on his way out the window. A shot was heard, but no bullet left the gun. It turned out to be a so-called "bummer", a bullet that got stuck in the gun tube, something that happens maybe once in ten thousand. So more people were lucky that time.

It turned out that the weapon was loaded, because they had forgotten to take the ammunition from the technical personnel.

When all was done and peace and quiet had returned to the airbase, Danielsen got his "bummer", and I think he wears it around his neck as an amulet.

Soon afterwards, there appeared a long article in the newspaper, "Stockholms-Tidningen", about Flight Mechanic Ljungström receiving a merit plaque from the head of F3, for his quick intervention against the crew of a foreign aircraft. Ljungström had thrown himself on the pilot and twisted the gun out of his hand, and also prevented the pilot from setting the aeroplane on fire!

Carlo and Elsa arrived in Karslborg with their few possessions just a few days before Monday, November 20, the day that Carlo had to report for duty at F6. They had been allocated a home in the town. It was not uncommon for the Danish pilots to live outside the airbases and pass in and out as duty required. Karlsborg is a small town which is beautifully located on the western shore of Lake Vättern. The town is the gateway into the western part of the 190 km-long Göta Canal. Today, Karlsborg has a population of just under 7,000, but in the nineteen-forties it was only about 4,000. However, the city had gained some importance during the nineteenth century, when the Karlsborg Fortress was constructed. According to the thinking of the time, it attained the status of being "the backup capital of Sweden", whereto the royal family, the government, the parliament, the

State Bank's gold supply and the crown regalia would be moved during wartime.

Just south of the Karlsborg Fortress, a new airbase was built in 1939, Västgöta Air Base – F6, which operated until 1994. After a pause of thirteen years, the Defence Department again took over the area and re-instated the military airport in 2007. But in early 1939 the airfield was only 1,600 x 1,200 metres, with two crossed paths functioning as runways. Among the buildings, there were a large hangar housing two divisions, and a building for the airbase's workshop. Special permission was required for access to the base area, and a permit to the airbase was issued to Carlo on November 21.

Karlsborg in the forties

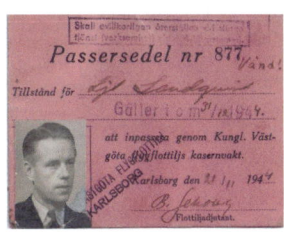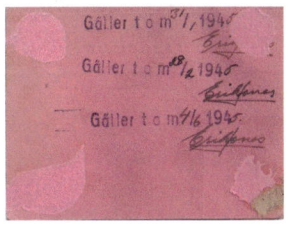

Carlo's permit to the F6 airbase in Karlsborg

Just two days later, Carlo was again sitting in an aeroplane with the engine roaring at full speed – the first time in four years. The aircraft was an Sk. 12 (School aeroplane 12, Focke-Wulf FW 44 Stieglitz) and Carlo was in the plane as "e.d.k." –

"student with double control" – under the watchful eye of Second Lieutenant Holmström. After only 25 minutes of landing exercises, he took over as lone pilot and ended the day with a twenty-minute flight performance over the F6 airfield, during which he demonstrated his skills in aerobatics.

The four Danish pilots at F6 Karlsborg in front of a B5 dive-bomber, late winter 1945. From left: Lieutenant C. H. Sandqvist, Lieutenant Captain E. B. Meincke, Lieutenant E. Møller, and Lieutenant D. C. W. Knudsen

It would now be two weeks before Carlo got back into an aeroplane, this time in a B5 bomber, a light American Northrop-Douglas DB-8A-1 which was licensed in Sweden. This time he conducted a 25-minute series of landing drills, again as e.d.k. student with Lieutenant Lönnberg as supervisor. A week later he took over as a pilot in the B5 plane. In the following months, he practiced individual flying, formation flying, blind flying, diving and shooting with the B5. Dropping bombs, however, was not included in the exercises yet, but that would come. The B5 plane was considered to be an ideal dive-bomber.

Aiming at a bomb target on the ground, by plunging the plane downwards at an angle of 60 degrees, was a method of attack that the Swedish Air Force employed to a large extent. There was a saying at the time that "the cradle of dive-bombing was in Sweden, and the Americans developed it, but it was the Germans who applied it".

Time passed quickly and Christmas, 1944, approached. It was time to take a little break from the Air Unit's exercises, and Carlo and Elsa were planning a reunion with their newly-found Danish friends from the Tingsryd area. A few days before Christmas Eve, they went to Möckelsnäs, where Pedro Gauguin and the other Danes had also arrived to celebrate the holiday.

Christmas is a special time for families to gather. But that was impossible for Carlo and Elsa this year. Their thoughts crossed the Kattegatt to Aalborg, where their sons had been left behind. How was life going on for Aage and the baby, whom they didn't even get to name before the flight to Sweden? How were the children's daily activities affected by the German occupation? When would they see their children again?

From Aage's perspective, it was not too bad. He suffered no distress, because his Grandma and Grandpa had a small farm that could produce a lot of food. He also did not find it strange to be sent to the bakery to buy "good cream". "Good cream" was actually whipping cream, the sale of which, like butter, was forbidden, because the Germans usurped these for transport to Germany. At home one could talk about "whipping cream", and Aage's Grandma would use it to make butter. But in the store, Aage was cautious and asked for "good cream".

However, the fact that the Germans were there was evident. There was often air alarm – Aalborg Airport was a target for British aerial bombings, and Gug, where the farm was located, was only 10 km southeast of the airport. During an air alarm, Aage would huddle in his Grandma's arms in the windowless hall, or sometimes down in the vegetable cellar. It happened once that a British aeroplane was shot down by the Germans and crashed just a kilometre away; but Aage was not allowed to see it, although the adults talked a lot about it.

Christmas Eve came, but the warm atmosphere, that his Grandma and Grandpa created for Aage, could not prevent the longing for his parents, which flourished more than usual this evening. While Aage was playing on the floor with a truck, a nice Christmas present, Aage's Grandpa sat and turned on the radio to get Sweden. A live broadcast of Swedish choral music filled the living room. Aage's Grandpa then suddenly said: "Aage, come over here to the radio. If you listen really care-fully, you can hear your mother and father singing all the way from Sweden". Aage went over to the radio and put his ear to the speaker. From that day to the present, he is still convinced that he actually heard his mother and father's voices in the choir. His Grandma said: "This is a Christmas Eve which we will never forget". No truer words were ever spoken!

There was not much exchange of letters between Danish refugees in Sweden and their relatives in Denmark. The only sign of life from Aalborg, that reached Carlo and Elsa in Karls-borg, arrived at the end of January, 1945. It was sent by Knud Hansen, the friend, who along with his wife Helga, had taken over the youngest son before the escape to Sweden. German censorship was severe – letters were opened and read, and many letters never arrived, even though false names were used for both the sender and recipient. But the letter from Aalborg was much appreciated and reassured Carlo and Elsa that both their children were doing well!:

<u>*Best friend*</u>   *Aalborg   20-1-1945*

I am writing to you, because it seems that you have entirely forgotten us. We have actually sent letters a couple of times; but you have been very busy. You are probably out in the woods at this time of the year, I imagine. But you should find the letter when you return.

We are otherwise fine, everyone here in Aalborg. The children are healthy and enjoy themselves. We are earning well, eat and drink well, what more can you ask for. We send with this letter a few pictures of the little boy, whom you have not seen, he turned 5 months yesterday, does he not look good? My brother-in-law has moved, they have rented out the old apartment [Carlo and Elsa's old apartment], *it's probably not that difficult either. I'll write another time (if we hear from you then)?*

Now the best regards with the hope of good health for you, from Birgitha and the children and me,

<u>*Rudolf.*</u>

Note. You should enlarge the picture where he appears in full length, remember that he is named after you. (Gösta).

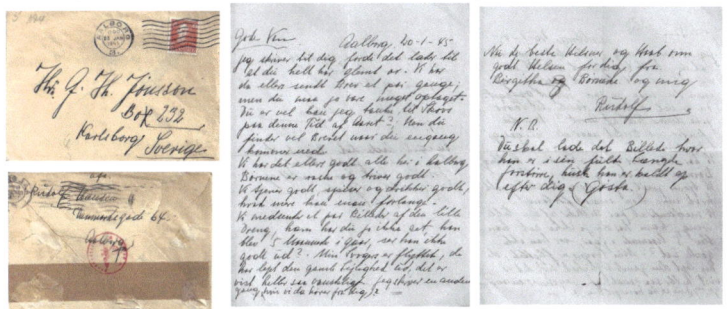

Knud Hansen's letter to Carlo, January, 1945, "approved" by the German censor (see the German stamp on the back of the envelope)

Knud had written "G. H. Jönsson" as a false Swedish name for Carlo on the front of the envelope, but the address in Sweden was correct. He himself signed the letter with "Rudolf" which also stood for the sender on the back of the envelope. The mentioning of the woods is probably Knud's way of misleading the German censorship. The letter also does not say that the mentioned child is the addressee's son – all to deceive the censorship, which succeeded since the letter arrived.

Now the youngest son had finally been given a name – Gösta – a Swedish name! And it was Knud and Helga who gave it to him.

Flight training with the B5 aircraft was resumed on January 10 and continued during January and February. Back in Karlsborg, after the Christmas festivities in Möckelsnäs, Carlo and Elsa had celebrated New Year's Eve and the beginning of the significant new year, 1945. A slightly delayed Christmas present arrived by mail in mid-January. It came from the Systemaktiebolaget in Skövde, the Motboks department, and it informed Carlo that from now on he could buy two litres of alcohol a month. (This Swedish alcohol purchase permit, however, lasted only until June 30, 1945. But by then the war would be over and Carlo would be able go to the local grocery store in Denmark as usual and buy as much as he wanted, whenever he wanted).

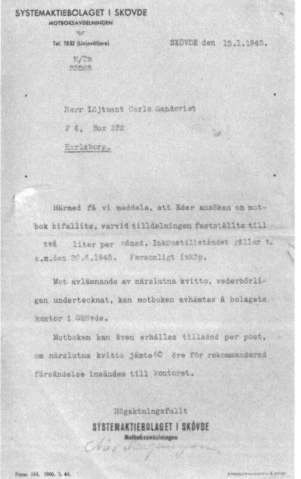

Carlo's alcohol purchase permit approved

A time limit of only three flight hours per month for the Danish pilots had been ordered by the head of the Swedish Air Staff – but this was not followed, however. For example, Carlo registered 2 hours and 45 minutes as pilot on B5 in January, and in February this became a full 4 hours and 5 minutes. On his 35-year birthday, February 28, he was also allowed to fly for three hours as a pilot in a B4 aircraft, where he performed "sausage flight", or more specifically target flight. In a sausage flight, the aircraft tows an aerial target, that looks like a giant sausage, at which units on the ground can aim their cannons during an exercise. The B4 plane was a double-decker Hawker Hart aircraft, which also could be used for dive bombing. That Carlo was allowed to fly this plane for three hours on his special day was probably a Swedish birthday present.

Although the leadership of the Danish Brigade appreciated the exercises with the B5 plane, some of the plane's short-comings were noticeable. One common experience was how the plane could behave during a careless landing: it tended to perform a "ground loop", that is, a turnaround on the ground. One story relates: A pilot had just completed a landing on a grass field and one wheel penetrated the grass layer – a ground loop was the result whereby the aircraft continued the landing, but now with the tail first. The pilot later claimed that he now had to increase the gas flow to slow the plane down to a full stop. What the Danes really wanted was access to the pride of the Swedish Air Force, namely the country's modern home-made Saab B17 bomber aircraft. But no Danish pilot was allowed to fly this plane. That would have bent the Swedish neutrality policy concerning the presence of the Danish police force too far – the Germans would had a hard time swallowing that. Nevertheless, the Brigade's leadership conducted very active negotiations with General Axel Ljungdahl, the Swedish Commander of the Aviation Staff, to achieve this. That was the big Danish dream – B17 for the Danish Brigade's Air Unit!

A Saab B17 utilises its strength to perform Santa's job, 1944 – would the Christmas present contain a promise to the Danish Brigade for 1945? (The front of a party script at F6)

Chapter 11: SAAB 17, the First Aircraft Designed and Produced by Sweden

"B17"! For many people outside Sweden, this designation is reminiscent of the American four-engine Boeing B-17 Flying Fortress, used by United States Army Air Corps during the extensive bombing of Germany in World War II. But in Sweden, B17 is the designation of the country's pride from the 1940s, the first design and production of its own dive bomber – an achievement that can be compared to today's Gripen aircraft, a Swedish warplane which competes with the best in the world.

In the mid-1930s, the Swedish Air Force had only access to a light bomber, namely the Hawker Hart (Swedish designation: B4), which was already obsolete. At this time, the Defence Commission advocated the creation of a reconnaissance plane as a vital defence component. However, the new light bomber, Northrop 8A (B5), which was manufactured under licence in Sweden in the late 1930s, was not suitable as a reconnaissance plane due to poor visibility downwards. Also, the B5 could not be converted to a seaplane, a plane that can take off and land on water. The Defence Commission wanted an all-round aircraft that could perform a variety of missions: "medium-heavy bomber, torpedo launcher, long-range reconnaissance plane, as well as a light bomber, army and naval reconnaissance aircraft," including artillery. Those requirements would eventually lead to the emergence of the Saab B17.

Several competing groups worked on plans for a new aircraft that would satisfy the Defence Commission's requirements. These were AB Svenska Järnvägsverkstädernas Aeroplanavdelning (ASJA) in Linköping, which was formed in 1930, and Svenska Aeroplan Aktiebolaget (Saab) in Trollhättan, which was established in 1937. These two manufacturers created the new ASJA, which together with Bofors, subsequently formed the AB Förenade Flygverkstäder (AFF), also in 1937. However, this collaboration did not work out well. In March 1939, Saab was restructured entirely and took over ASJA. The development and construction departments were located in Linköping, and the production was divided between Linköping and Trollhättan.

In connection with the series production of the licensed American B5, some American engineers came to Linköping in the summer of 1938, where they contributed with their knowledge of project and construction work. Their expertise, including shell construction, was also useful in the planning of the B17, and in the summer of 1939 the number of American engineers in Linköping grew to 45. But it ended abruptly in September after Germany attacked Poland, when most of the Americans hurried back to the USA. The last three Americans left Sweden at the beginning of 1940. The planning of the B17 now continued with only the Swedish staff. Tests of different scale models were performed in the low-speed wind tunnel at the Royal Institute of Technology in Stockholm (KTH), supplemented with data from a high-speed wind tunnel at the California Institute of Technology (Caltech), in the USA. A prototype for the B17 was ready for its first flight on May 18, 1940.

The flight was performed by Saab's test pilot, Claes Smith, and became dramatic. The canopy blew off at takeoff and injured Smith's face, covering it in blood. He managed to carry out the test flight program, "one-eyed", as he said afterwards. After an extensive number of test flights and many design improvements, the B17 was finally approved for series production in December, 1940.

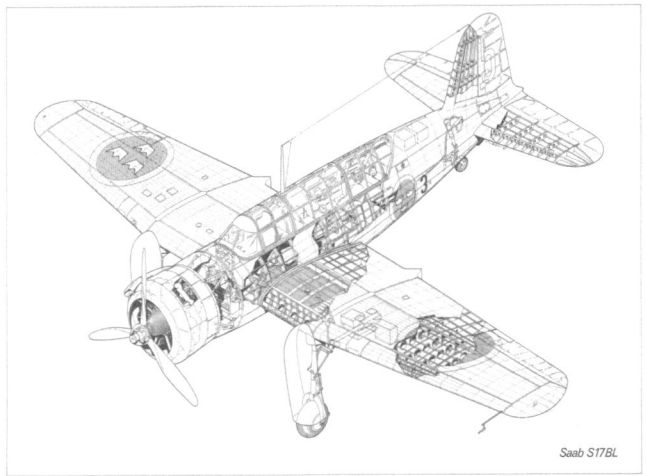

"X-ray" drawing of Saab S17 (Drawing: Saab, Stig Nilsson)

There was only one problem: the engine! The first prototype had an 880 hp Bristol Mercury XII engine. In the second prototype a 1065 hp Pratt & Whitney Twin Wasp C-3g (TW C-3) engine was installed. The TW C-3 engine was the preferred engine on the B17, and Saab had placed a large order on that engine in the US. After the outbreak of World War II, the US revoked all of those orders and did not allow licensed manufacturing of the engine in Sweden. However, NOHAB Flygmotor in Trollhättan was given disposal to one TW C-3 engine and was commissioned by the Swedish Aviation Administration to make copies of it. Success! The pirated engine was labelled as STW C-3. It was a formidable achievement which, however, took a long time. Deliveries of the STW C-3 engine to Saab did not begin until March, 1944, and further deliveries of the finished B17s, with STW C-3 engines, to the

Swedish Air Force began in May, 1944. The re-engined version of the B17 was designated the B17A.

In the meantime, Saab produced the B17 with other variants of engines. For example, licensed Bristol Mercury XXIV (My XXIV) engines with 980 hp were delivered to Saab. This less powerful engine was installed in the B17 as early as in the turn of the year 1941/42, and these aircraft were designated as B17B. Moreover, the 1020 hp Piaggio P XI (P XI) engines were purchased from Italy in the spring of 1943. But the Piaggio engines were of lower technical standard and had inherent design flaws. These aircraft were designated B17C. A total of 325 B17 aircraft were built, of which 133 were the B17A, 115 the B17B and 77 the B17C variant.

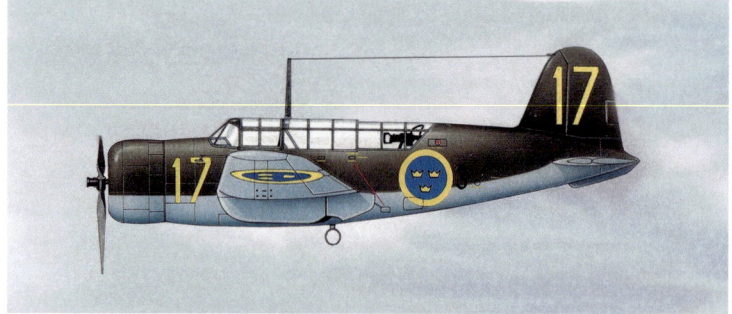

Profile image of B17B. The small black number behind the Swedish Air Force logo indicates the airbase, in this case F3 Malmslätt. Note the (black) movable machine gun under the openable canopy over the spotter seat. (Saab, Hans Kampf)

A significant improvement in the B17 compared to the B5 was the retractable landing gear, including the tail wheel. The B5 was equipped with a fixed landing gear, which reduced the air speed due to the increased drag. The characteristic wheel fairings on the B17 improved the aerodynamic properties of the aircraft when the wheels were in the retracted position. But the fairings also had the opposite function in the gear-extended position as a speed brake during dive-bomb operations. For winter operations the landing gear could be replaced by skis. The ski structures were also retractable, a world-unique design. Since the B17 should also be capable of sea reconnaissance, a sea-plane version with floats was developed; however, the floats were not retractable.

Maximum takeoff mass for the B17 was 4,200 kg and the empty mass, 2,650 kg. The maximum speed was 444, 395 and 433 km/h for the B17A, B17B and B17C, respectively, and 345 km/h for the sea version. The maximum range was about 1,800 km for the land versions. The ceiling was between 7,000 and 9,500 m, and the cruise speed between 290 and 370 km/h. The takeoff distance was 375 m, and landing distance was between 275 and 300 m.

The weaponry of the B17 consisted of machine guns and bombs. Two 8 mm machine guns were mounted in the outer wings and a rear-facing movable 8 mm machine gun in the tail gunners compartment under an openable canopy. In the belly, there was an openable compartment for a 500 kg or 250 kg bomb, that could be lifted out by a fork lift to deploy the bomb below the propeller in the dive-bombing maneuver. Alternatively, five 50-kg explosives or bombs could be carried in the bomb compartment. In addition, four 50-kg bombs could be mounted under the wings. It was also possible to replace the 50-kg bombs with 12-kg explosives or 6-kg firebombs in capsules of 3 bombs each. Dummy bombs weighing 250, 50 or 8 kg could be installed instead of active bombs. All in all, the B17 was able to meet the extensive requirements for an all-round warplane that the Defence Commission had demanded.

Moreover, an ultra-modern bomb sight was developed for

the B17, and installed on the nose in front of the windscreen. In a bomb operation, the pilot selected the dive angle and the entry altitude. With the fixed bomb sight, he aimed the plane at the target and pressed the bomb release lever. The exact time for opening the bomb door was automatically calculated by a gyro-stabilized central instrument. As input data, the aircraft mass, ambient air pressure (which determined the altitude of the bomb release), wind speed and direction, airspeed and acceleration were used. The bomb release action took place at the pullup. After a long development period, the bomb sight showed surprisingly high accuracy.

The first batch of B17As was delivered to the Swedish Air Force base at F6 in Karlsborg in July, 1943. However, they did not have the Swedish-made STW C-3 engines, which unfortunately only were available a year later. According to the first plans, fourteen B17As without engines would be shipped by sea to the quay in Karlsborg for further transport by land to the F6 Karlsborg base, where they would await the completion of the Swedish STW C-3 engines. But fortunately, Saab got hold of some French TW C-3 engines, so that the first B17A aircraft were able to arrive by air to F6 Karlsborg – a much more dignified manner. Already by the end of August, 1943, there were a sufficient number of B17As at F6 Karlsborg to operate in units of nine aircraft. However, it would take until the summer of 1944 before F6 Karlsborg was fully equipped with B17.

During the post-war period, the B17 was initially an essential component of the Swedish Air Force. But after the reorganization of the Swedish defence system in 1947, the Air Force's priority shifted from light bombers, such as B17, to fighter aircraft as a result of experiences of the war years. The

*B17A divisions lined up at F6 Karlsborg on a public show in
1945, shortly after the end of World War II. Note the visiting
American B-17 Flying Fortress in the lower-left corner of the
picture. (Photo: Karlsborg Fortress Museum -
donation album by K-A Hansson)*

previous bomber bases were transformed into air-fighter bases,
with North American P-51 Mustangs, and the new Saab J 21A
aircraft. The redundant and fully functional B17C aircraft were
either scrapped or used as firing targets. However, many of the
B17As served until the mid-fifties for towing of shooting
targets, staff transports, weather observation, etc. One B17A
continued in civilian service, towing targets on the island of
Gotland until June 30, 1968 – its designation was SE-BYH and
it was flown by a woman pilot. Moreover, 46 B17A aircraft
were sold to Ethiopia between 1947 and 1953, where they were
the backbone of the Ethiopian Air Force. As recently as 1970,

some B17A aircraft were still flying in Ethiopia. One B17A is preserved at the Air Force Museum in Linköping. In 1970, Sweden presented a B17A to Denmark as a gift to commemorate the Danish Brigade's Air Unit in Sweden 25 years earlier – it is now on display at the Technical Museum of Denmark in Elsinore.

In Sweden, one B17A aircraft is still (2021) in flying condition. It is the SE-BYH, which was restored by enthusiasts at Saab to an airworthy condition for Saab's 60th anniversary in 1997. The idea of restoring the aircraft was born at a dinner at the "rollout" of the Saab 39B Gripen two years earlier. The ready-to-fly B17A was painted in the colours of the time, and the number 7, beside the Swedish Air Force logo, is symbolic of the Air Force base F7 Såtenäs – where the Danish Brigade's Air Unit gathered on May 4 - 5, 1945!

Saab B17A and Gripen (Photo: Saab)

Chapter 12: B17 to the Danes at F6 Karlsborg, 1945

Carlo leaned back in the cockpit of the B4, quite pleased. The three-hour towing flight on his birthday had gone well: no artillery fire from the ground had struck his B4, but kept to the target (the "sausage"), pulled behind the plane. Now it was time for a small party lunch with colleagues and then home to continue the celebration with Elsa.

Birthday party for 35-year-old Carlo with the Danish F6 flight colleagues. At the end of the table from the left: Lieutenant E. Møller, Lieutenant C. H. Sandqvist (with sunglasses), Lieutenant Captain E. B. Meincke and Lieutenant D. C. W. Knudsen

War exercises with B4 and B5 were OK. But what about B17A, which were plentiful at F6 Karlsborg at this time? On the day before, Carlo had been allowed to sit in a B17 for the first time. He acted as the signaller in the spotter's seat behind the Swedish pilot during a half-hour bombing exercise. In March, there were another couple of 30 to 40 minute B17 flights as signaller on bombing and bearing training flights. Officially, it was still not entirely accepted to have Danish pilots as passengers on B17 flights, but changes were under-way. On March 16, 1945, the Swedish Deputy Chief of Staff of the Swedish Air Force, K. J. A. Silfverberg issued a classified order document (Air Force H76: "Special provisions for Danish personnel in the line of duty on airbases"), which was sub-mitted to the Commanders of F4, F6, F11 and F12 depots, with effect on April 1, 1945. Paragraph 7 of this document states:

7. The duties of aircraft mechanics include:
a) Service as a mechanic on aircraft B5 and B17
b) The person in question is granted the right to accompany aircraft during flight assignments as a passenger at own risk

On April 14, 1945 another classified order was issued by the Chief of Staff, A. Ljungdahl: Air Force H96/45: "Rehearsal course for Danish personnel", and sent to the same airbase commanders:

1. The purpose of the course is to familiarize the students with the B17 aircraft, preferably B17C, if possible, so that they can serve as pilots in military units, or second mechanics on the aircraft type.
2. Dates for the training: at F 4, F 6 and F 12 April 19 - May 11, at F 7 May 2 - May 26.
3. Students: staff at the relevant airbase with the exception of F 11, whose staff takes the course at F 7.
4. Flight time: maximum 25 hours per pilot.

5. _Bomb distribution_: 50 8-kg dummy bombs – and two heavy (50-kg and 250-kg) dummy bombs, corresponding to one full bomb load per student.

6. _Ammunition_: 500 8-mm so-called bullets (one fourth with tracking light trails) per student.

7. Flight equipment is provided at the airbase.

8. The Air Force's regulations and safety rules for flight, bombing and shooting must be observed. The students' preferences on the training should be met as far as possible. However, the students' previous training and experience should be taken into account. The requirements for flight safety must not be neglected.

9. A brief _report_ on the training results should be submitted to the Chief of the Air Force after the end of the training.

10. The training mainly includes

Flight: Repetition of current regulations and safety rules

    Pilot instructions

    Normal flight and advanced flight applicable to the air team's tactics

    Group and division flight

Equipment knowledge:

    Knowledge of aircraft B17, to the required extent

Shooting (with aircraft weapons): Knowledge of equipment

    Safety instructions

    Preparatory exercises, classroom exercises and application training according to SIF II to the extent that the depot Chief decides, among other things, according to the stu-dents' educational level

Bombing: Knowledge of equipment

    Safety instructions

    Preparatory exercises, classroom exercises and appli-

cation training according to HIF II to the extent that the depot Chief decides, among other things, according to the students' educational level.

Signal service: Knowledge of signal equipment and its use in aircraft B17.

Exercise in signal service in collaboration with Swedish-speaking signalling parties.

Now it was finally over, the fight to make B17 available to the Danish Brigade's Air Unit. Santa's promise from 1944 was fulfilled. At the same time, the flight time as a pilot was increased from 3 hours to a full 25 hours per month for the Danish pilots. The development of the war had rapidly improved for the Allies. The Germans were facing a total defeat, and Sweden now fully dared to take a stand for its Nordic neighbours.

On Thursday April 19, 1945, the same day as this ordinance came into force at F6 Karlsborg, Carlo sat behind the controls on a B17A with the designation "K" on the fin – as "edk: student under double command". The spotter seat, behind him, was occupied by a Swedish pilot. A 10-minute flight was performed. After that, Carlo took over completely as "ff.: flying pilot" and made two approach training flights, lasting 25 minutes. Finally, the Swedish pilot left Carlo alone in his B17A - "K" ready for his solo flight. During the next 40 minutes, he completed three flights and successfully performed arrets (so-called pincer manoeuvres), steep dive and landing training. Very pleased with himself, he then reported to his Danish group leader, Lieutenant Captain Meincke, who had carefully followed the program from the ground with the landing flag in his hand.

*Carlo makes the last landing at F6 Karlsborg during his
solo flight with B17A - "K", April 19, 1945*

*Lieutenant Sandqvist reports his solo flight with B17A - "K"
to the Danish group leader at F6 Karlsborg, Lieutenant
Captain Meincke (with the landing flag)*

*A few pages from Carlo's logbook from the flights with B17
at F6 in April 1945*

Now followed an intense period with Carlo as the pilot on
B17 flights to practice shooting, bombing, group flying, tactical
attacks and diving. The bombing took place on a bomb target
area by the lake Vättern near the F6 base in Karlsborg. The
normal bombing procedure was to dive at a pitch angle of 60 to
70 degrees. This was done at a high speed, while the signaller
in the spotter's seat called out the altitude to help the pilot level
out in time after the bomb was released. How did it feel then to

be part of such a diving attack? In a newspaper article in the autumn of 1945, a journalist described his experience of sitting behind the pilot in a B17 bomb attack:

We are hanging right under the lower side of the cloud banks, and 1,500 metres below us is the TARGET, a collection of tanks in a large bog. And so we start the dive. The nose is pointed towards the ground. The engine noise increases to a roar. Even though you know that you are securely tied in, you grasp tightly onto the seat. There is buzzing in the ears, the oxygen mask hangs straight down, and through the bottom windows you see 8 small lumps, which fall to the ground ap-proximately parallel to the plane. While the passenger in the back seat convulsively holds on and tries to gather his senses, the pilot, cool as a cucumber, has been waiting for the right moment to drop the 50-kilo bombs towards his predetermined part of the target. Some fantastic moments during the dive: At 900 meters you have a feeling that your body is being pushed backwards and downwards, and that we are rising straight upwards. The pilot has levelled the plane. But only for a few moments. Immediately afterwards, we are on our way down again. And now we see the ground, which had not been thought about so much earlier when it was at a safe distance, come rushing up towards you at a speed of 400 km per hour, or about 110 meters per second. .... it buzzes in the ears, it twists, it tears and jerks and heels and thunders in the plane. And then, all of a sudden, you are pushed back again. And when you recover, the plane is in a narrow right turn, at about 50 meters above the ground.

In April, 1945, in addition to the four Danish pilots (E. B.

Meincke, D. K. W. Knudsen, E. Møller and Carlo), F6 Karlsborg also had four Danish aircraft mechanics, H. K. Jensen, A. G. Johansen, C. Møller and Øst-Møller. All eight Danes now had full access to the B17 plane and the training progressed rapidly. Courses in signal service and handling of bombs and weapons were given to the Danes by their Swedish colleagues. Carlo also held a navigation course for the other participants. Similar education and training on the B17 aircraft by Danish pilots and technical staff also took place at the other two airbases, where the Danish Brigade's Air Unit was located, F4 Östersund and F12 Kalmar. Now it was only a matter of the Danes forming one coherent unit out of the three groups. But was Sweden now ready to provoke the Germans and "Save Denmark"?

*The Swedish
division leader at F6,
B. Paulsen*

*The Danish
group leader at F6,
E.B. Meincke*

Chapter 13: The Swedish Plan to "Save Denmark"

On Tuesday, September 12, 1944, a four-page handwritten letter was sent with a cry for help from a Danish to a Swedish citizen. The Swedish recipient was Professor Gösta Bagge, a member of the Second Chamber of the Swedish Parliament, the party leader for the Conservative Party and Minister of Ecclesiastical Affairs in the Swedish coalition government. The Danish sender was Ole Bjørn Kraft, a highly ranked politician in the Conservative People's Party and a member of the Danish Parliament since 1926. He would eventually become Minister of Defence in the Danish Liberation Government in 1945 and later Minister of Foreign Affairs. The letter is preserved in the Swedish National Archives and the first page of the message is:

OLE BJØRN KRAFT   KØBENHAVN K. VENDERSGADE 28   12/9-44.

Kære Gösta Bagge.

Situationen i Danmark er nu meget anspændt. Befrielsen af en Række okkuperede Lande har vakt Forventning om, at vor Time opgaa nærmer sig. Hvis den Situation skulde komme til at prætippe, at Modstanden her i Landet gaar over til aktion inten paa Grund af Invasion eller af andre Grunde, vil der for os rejse sig et meget vigtigt Spørgsmaal. Som du ved, er der i nogen Tid blevet uddannet saakaldte Politisoldater paa svensk Grund. Det var oprindelig Tanken, at de

The whole letter reads:

Dear Gøsta Bagge.

The situation in Denmark is now very tense. The liberation of many occupied countries has aroused the expectation that our time is also approaching. If the situation should arise that the resistance in this country turns into action, either because of invasion or for other reasons, a very important question will arise for us. As you know, so-called police soldiers have been trained on Swedish soil for some time. It was originally intended that they should first take up action as law enforcers, when the Germans were well out of the country. But if we get into a hard fight for life and death beforehand, it will feel completely unreasonable for both them and us, that they should be inactive spectators, all the more so as their presence in Denmark will perhaps be of crucial significance. This is only a conceivable possibility. But should there arrive a request from the responsible political party in Denmark to the Swedish Government, to allow the <u>immediate</u> departure of these people, or should the question be raised before you in a different way – which perhaps already has happened – you must know that it also occurs on behalf of the Conservative People's Party. For the sake of the Nordic countries and our future, the Party, and Tibiger and I, ask you to support such a request with all the authority that you have at your disposal. I clearly see all the objections that can be raised from a Swedish Neutrality policy viewpoint. Still, by responding positively to such a possible request, Sweden will render its brotherland a service, that will live in Danish hearts throughout all time and contribute more to Nordic co-operation, through such a simple action, than can be accomplished in any other way.

We live a dangerous life in Denmark at the moment, but we are in good spirits, and full of hope and faith in a better future for the Nordic countries, and for us.

The most heartfelt greetings from
Yours sincerely
Ole Bjørn Kraft.

This letter was received by Bagge just over a week after an important meeting with the Swedish ministers, where the matter in Kraft's letter had been dealt with in detail. The question had been raised, following a petition from the informal but actual Danish prime minister, the Social Democrat Vilhelm Buhl. This is clear from Gösta Bagge's notes, which are also preserved in the Swedish National Archives. An excerpt follows below:

Sept. 4 [1944] Prime Minister's Office.
.... Then [P.E.] Sköld [the Swedish Social Democratic Minister of Defence] presented a petition from... Buhl on the purchase of bullets, which was granted, and the question of permission for the Danes to get the trained so-called police force, with weapons, transported to Denmark, as soon as the legal authorities in Denmark so requested. P.A. [Hanson, the Swedish Social Democratic Prime Minister] endorsed; I wanted to think about the matter, as this was contrary to the whole position so far. It was an extremely important decision and a complete step away from our policy so far. The Foreign Affairs Committee should be consulted. [C.] Günther [the Swedish Independent Foreign Minister] agreed with me. The fact was that we had always made it a condition for the training of Danish and Norwegian police, that they should not be allowed to go back to their countries until the Germans had been expelled

from the country, and then to maintain order. Now the purpose would apparently be something completely different, namely that these so-called policemen, who were in fact trained military troops, would be used together with the partisans to drive out the Germans. It was reported, however, that an invasion of Denmark was probably expected around 15 Sept. and that the Danes then needed this reinforcement. It was decided that we would wait a bit with the decision, in order to think more about the matter and learn all the details.

It was a week after this meeting that Bagge received the letter from Kraft, his conservative colleague in Denmark, who emphasized the need for help to Denmark. And now the course of events in Denmark continued to affect Swedish views: the Germans' massive action, a few days later on September 19, when they disbanded the Danish police force and sent many of the policemen to the Buchenwald concentration camp. On the next day, the first presentation of a very preliminary plan to "Save Denmark" (RD – Rädda Danmark) was held before the Swedish Commander-in-Chief (ÖB – Överbefälhavaren), General H. Jung. However, this plan remained an internal matter for the Swedish Defence Staff until February, 1945, when ÖB informed the Swedish government of the plan's existence. But the first real RD presentation to the government did not take place until April 5, 1945, when it also received the approval of the Minister of Defence, Sköld. A few days later, intensive detailed planning began at the Defence Staff, as well as at the Military Staff, the Air Force Staff and the Navy Staff.

Developments in Denmark had led to this turnaround within the Swedish government. The threatening, but absent, Allied invasion of Jutland's west coast in September, 1944, had increased the support for aid to Denmark. However, during the winter of 1944/45, the advance of the Allied troops towards Germany was slower than expected, and the RD plane went into hibernation. At the same time, the Soviet Union had great successes, and fear arose that the Red Army would be the first to reach Denmark, which would then become a scene for a bloody battle between Russian and German troops. If that would happen, it could activate Danish communist resistance groups and result in chaos. During January - February, 1945, it also appeared that large German troops would move up through Denmark. Furtermore, a new German Commander-in-chief came to Denmark, General Lindemann, who was a strongly devoted and loyal Nazi. He promised a fight to the last man in an isolated Denmark, even after the war situation for the Germans became utterly hopeless. In such a situation, the Danish resistance movement, in connection with a possible transfer of the Danish Brigade from Sweden to Denmark, would hardly be able to maintain order on its own. Therefore, the need for Swedish intervention to "Save Denmark" grew significantly. The Danish viewpoint was not a demand for Sweden to enter the war, but rather only to make an effort in the final stages of the war, when Germany was in military and political disintegration.

Although the official position of the Swedish government still prevented a direct intervention in Denmark, a plan to Save Denmark was ready for activation in April, 1945. The RD plan was primarily to secure Zealand and Bornholm (the Danish island in the Baltic), and possibly later also Funen. But Jutland, especially with the important German airbase, Aalborg Airport, was not included! The operation against Zealand was to be carried out quickly with a large combat force: the 3rd Army

Corps of two divisions, a motorized and an armoured brigade, together with light naval forces, and the major part of the Air Force. The Air Force included about 300 aircraft, divided into a fighter squadron consisting of five flotillas, a bomber squadron of four flotillas and several divisions of reconnaissance aircraft. The fighter squadron was responsible for protection over the Sound, and the bomber squadron could quickly be deployed against German naval vessels and resistance pockets on Zealand. During a regular war operation against Zealand, one could also expect efforts from the Allied side. Of course, the Danish Brigade, with its 4,744 men (number for March 7, 1945), and the Danish naval flotilla, which had fled to Sweden in 1943, would take part in the operation. However, there was no mention in the RD plan of the Danish Brigade's small Air Unit, possibly because it did not have its own equipment on hand, and only consisted of about twenty pilots and technicians. Parts of this Air Unit, however, had developed their own plans – with a focus on northern Jutland, especially Aalborg Airport. It was all this political and military development during April, 1945, that made Sweden finally give the Danish pilots access to the B17 aircraft.

On Friday, May 4, 1945, the Swedish Chief of the Defence Staff, C. A. Ehrensvärd, sent the following "Basic Regulations for Operation RD" to the Military Commander of the I. Military Area, Major General A.E.W. af Klercker, with a request to submit in person a report on the main objectives of the planning before May 11:

SECRET Belongs to Headquarters Defence Staff No. H 34:2, May 4, 1945.

Basic rules for Operation RD.

A. *General.*

The development of events in Denmark may go in such a direction that a Swedish military (police) intervention may become relevant. This would primarily be intended to ensure public order until the time when legal Danish authorities could completely take over this task, as well as to disarm and detain German units.

The intervention would primarily aim to pacify Zealand and Bornholm. Due to the lack of, among other things, modern disembarkation equipment, undertakings with the above goals will only be carried out if it can be assumed with certainty that the German armed forces' will to resist is significantly reduced. Even if this condition is met, one must be prepared to encounter armed resistance in some places. Intervention must therefore be planned and carried out as military operations, so that any resistance can be subdued.

For the operation against _Zealand_ (Själland) (RD_S_), this will be carried out by the 3rd Army Corps, naval forces, fixed and mobile coastal artillery, and the main part of the Air Force. The Danish police troops in Sweden and Danish vessels, detained here, will also participate.

The operation against _Bornholm_ (RD_B_) is carried out by naval forces, together with an infantry regiment and local defence unit from Defence Area 15, and supported by an air combat force. Only on the condition that resistance from naval and air combat forces is judged to be almost non-existent, will this operation be carried out _at the same time_ as the operation against Zealand, otherwise later.

Remote protection for the operations against Zealand and Bornholm is prepared by the main part of the fleet.

As information to troops, officers and the Danish civilian population, the following will be sent out later:

> *"Guide lines for the soldier"*
> *"Guide lines for the officer"*
> *"Call to the people of Denmark".*

B. Provisions for Operation RDS.
I. Task and leadership.

1. The <u>task</u> is to pacify Zealand and to prepare for the pacification of Mön, Falster and Lolland, as well as Funen and Langeland.

2. The <u>leadership</u> is exercised by the Chief of the 3rd Army Corps. Together with the Chief of Marines (CM) regarding remote protection, Chief of the Air Force (CFV) aerial support.

II. Armed forces at the disposal of the 3rd Army Corps.

3. The following combat forces are intended to be <u>subordinated</u> to Chief of Corps:

> *a) 3. corps staff reinforced with personnel from Coastal Artillery (KA) according to CM decision,*
>
> *b) land forces in accordance with Appendix 1,*
>
> *c) naval forces in accordance with Appendix 2,*
>
> *d) two aircraft type S 14, a TMR IX and some fighters by agreement with CFV,*
>
> *e) branch of fortifications (BRB) according to Appendix 3 (later),*
>
> *f) voluntary fire brigades in accordance with Appendix 4 (later),*
>
> *g) Danish police force in accordance with Appendix 5.*

III. Special instructions.

4. *Instructions for the operation's military planning.*

The planning shall primarily include disembarkation on Zealand and occupation of this island.

The landing is planned in two alternatives:

Alt I:

Attack on Copenhagen, Rungsted and Elsinore areas with concentration of forces against Elsinore.

Alt II: = Alt I, however, that the attack on the Copenhagen area is limited to diversive operations.

Alternatives are determined by Commander-in-Chief depending on the knowledge of the enemy's resistance capacity.

In the first place, the ports necessary for own communications will be taken, mainly Elsinore, in the second place Copenhagen and other major ports as well as airports and essential traffic hubs.

German destruction operations, as well as the transport of troops, equipment and Danish hostages, must be counteracted. Instructions for occupying a place are given in Appendix 6 (later).

5. *Instructions for administration.*

In principle, all civil administrative tasks are handled by Danish authorities.

The military territorial command is exercised by the corps commander; co-operation is sought with Danish military territorial officers. All connections with Danish authorities and with the Danish public are made, if possible, through Danish officers or Danish liaison staff.

Additional instructions for administration will be issued later.

6. _Instructions for the participation of Danish police personnel, trained in Sweden, and by the resistance movement in Denmark._

The majority of the Danish police troops are held together and are expected to be placed under Danish command at an early stage after disembarkation. Personnel from the police troops are assigned to the Swedish units as staff personnel, land guides and shipping pilots.

For collaboration with the police troops and the resistance movement in Denmark, Danish staff personnel will be made available to the Swedish corps commander.

IV. Remote protection at sea.

7. *For remote protection at sea, CM is responsible with the majority of the fleet.*

V. Air support.

8. *The main part of the Air Force, under the command of the CFV, cooperates with the army corps during the landing operation.*

Aerial support after landing is dependent on the development of the situation.

Required details, regarding basing and intended operations, are sent by CFV directly to the commanders concerned.

VI. Air defense.

9. *Air surveillance in the liberated parts of Denmark is organized by the Chief of Corps, as soon as possible, in cooperation with the Danish authorities.*

If necessary, the Chief of Corps disposes of unor-

ganized air surveillance units within I. military district.

VII. Equipment for transhipment.
See Appendix 7 (later).

VIII. Intelligence.
See Appendix 8.

IX. Signal service.
See Appendix 9.

X. Maintenance service.
See Appendix 10.

C. Provisions for Operation RDB.
XI. Task and leadership
10.   The task is to <u>pacify</u> Bornholm.

11.   The <u>leadership</u> is exercised by CM. CFV cooperates with CM regarding air support.

XII. Combat forces at CM's disposal.
12.   The following <u>forces</u> are intended to participate:

a) naval forces according to CM decision.

b) land forces, subordinate to CM, in accordance with Appendix 11.

XIII. Special instructions.
13.   <u>Instructions for the operation's military planning.</u>

German destruction operations, as well as the transport of troops, equipment and Danish hostages, must be counteracted. Instructions for occupying a place are given in

Appendix 6 (later).

14. <u>*Instructions for administration.*</u>

In principle, all <u>civil</u> <u>administrative</u> <u>tasks</u> are handled by the Danish authorities.

The <u>military</u> <u>territorial</u> <u>command</u> is exercised by CM; cooperation is sought with Danish military territorial commanders. All connections with Danish authorities and with the Danish public are made, if possible, by Danish officers or Danish liaison staff.

Additional instructions for administration will be issued later.

15. For planning <u>collaboration with the resistance movement</u> on Bornholm, Danish staff personnel will be made available to CM.

XIV. Air support.

16. Air Force units, under CFV command, cooperate with the landing operation with CM.

XV. Air defense.

17. Air surveillance on Bornholm is organized through CM's responsibility, as soon as possible, in collaboration with the Danish authorities.

For this purpose, CM disposes of, if necessary, unorganized air surveillance units within Karlskrona region by direct agreement with the military officer of I. military district.

XVI. The maintenance service of the land forces.

See Appendix 12 (later).

D. Secrecy Provisions.

18.   *Planning and other preparations must take place under strict secrecy.*

Executives may be informed of part of the planning in advance only to the extent, that is indispensable for the operation to be carried out in accordance with this order. Civil authorities may only be informed after ÖB's consent.

Necessary correspondence takes place, until further notice, with <u>personalized</u> written missives.

E. Time conditions.

19. *Operation RD must be able to be <u>initiated</u> 8 days after order.*

Sweden would now, from May 4, 1945, fully commit itself to "Save Denmark". That same evening, however, the dramatic message came from Field Marshal Montgomery's headquarters in northern Germany: that the Germans had capitulated in Denmark (as well as in the Netherlands and northwestern Germany). The plan to "Save Denmark" was never put into action!

Chapter 14: The Plan for the Attack
on Aalborg Airport, 1945

Carlo and Elsa had now, after five months, achieved a kind of daily routine in Karlsborg where they lived. Every day, Carlo left Elsa and their home in the small town for the short trip out to the airbase. In the second half of April, 1945, there was a heavy activity among the Danish pilots and technicians, especially after they gained access to the B17 aircraft. During that period, Meincke performed 20 flights as a pilot on the B17 with a total flight time of 12 hours and 35 minutes, Knudsen 20 flights in 9 hours and 19 minutes, Møller 23 flights in 11 hours and 35 minutes and Carlo 23 flights in 12 hours and 5 minutes. They began to feel at home in the pilot seat on the B17. The Danish Lieutenant Captain V. Holm, who at this time was actually at F12 Kalmar, has described the feeling:

It [B17] *was outstanding. You sat in a huge cockpit, there was plenty of room for everything, the rear seat was superb, and the aeroplane was perfect for dive-bombing, ... it was equipped with an ultra-modern gyro-controlled bomb sight, that enabled the bomb to be released at the pullup .... there was a retractable gear .... and we had no accidents with that type of aircraft.*

What was the purpose of all this training? Did the Danish pilots know anything about the efforts that were taking place at a higher level, such as the "Save Denmark" plan? What were the hopes of the Command for Military Refugees, which was the Headquarters of the Danish Brigade in Stockholm? Its chief, Major General K. Knudtzon, who had been instrumental in gaining access to the B17 for the Danish pilots, realised that the Danish Brigade's Air Unit must conspire as a military unit with both the Swedish Air Force and, in a broader context, with the SHAEF (Supreme Headquarters Allied Expeditionary Forces) in Britain.

Negotiations with SHAEF, to have the Danish Brigade in Sweden recognised as a strategic reserve, began on a small scale as early as 1943. In April, 1944, the English Commander Hollingworth secretly visited Stockholm to investigate the issue of establishing a small Danish military staff at General Eisenhower's headquarters in Britain. In August, SHAEF invited the Danish journalist, Ebbe Munck, to London, where he should secure SHAEF's recognition of the Danish Brigade as a collaborating military unit. Munck was stationed in Stockholm and was a key figure in the contact between the British Special Operations Executive (SOE) and the Danish military intelligence service. The Danish Brigade was from now on named DANFORCE. There were also discussions about the Brigade's transfer to Denmark when the situation required it. In October, SHAEF formed a special department for planning Denmark's liberation and transition from German occupation to freedom and peace. This department, the "SHAEF Mission to Denmark", and whose head became Major General H. Dewing, consisted of about fifty British and American officers and officials. On November 7, 1944, five Danish officers from the army, navy and air force flew from Bromma Airport to Scotland on a Douglas DC-3 aircraft. From there they traveled further on to London, where they formed "The Danish Military Mission to SHAEF". Lieutenant Colonel Bjarkov represented the Danish Brigade's Air Unit in this mission.

Major General Dewing paid his first visit to Stockholm in

December, 1944, and negotiated with Major General Knudtzon on the position of the Danish Brigade within SHAEF. By this step, the Brigade, including the Air Unit, became a part of the Allied war machine. Dewing returned to Sweden on April 14, 1945, and reviewed the plan for the Brigade's activation with Knudtzon. When Field Marshal Montgomery's 21st Army Group in Northern Germany issued the "Yellow Light", a code, "Hans is sick", would be sent from Denmark to Sweden. This was the signal to activate the Brigade. In the case of an order for "Green Light", the Brigade's transfer to Denmark should be carried out immediately.

In parallel with the SHAEF development, Sweden's own "Save Denmark" RD plan continued. On April 27, 1945, the Chief of the Swedish Air Force, A. Ljungdahl, issued the following top-secret order (H21), for photographing the coast of Zealand, to Colonel H. Beckhammer at the F3 depot in Malmslätt:

Units from F 3 perform photography tasks as soon as possible, as follows.
1. Task:
Oblique pictures of the coastline (map 1: 300,000 no. D3):
Taarbaek (about 10 km north of Copenhagen) - Elsinore - Hornbaek (about 10 km west-northwest of Elsinore).
The primary section to be photographed: Vedbaek (10 km southwest of the island of Ven) - Elsinore - Hellebaek (6 km northwest of Elsinore).
2. The pictures are primarily intended as a basis for the planning of landing operations, and for the survey of defence preparations undertaken.

3. Photographs should be sent as soon as possible in 5 copies to the Chief of Air Staff, in person.

4. Danish territorial waters may not be overflown.

5. Force, camera equipment, etc. according to the depot head's decision.

6. Locating is arranged through the depot head by direct contact with the appropriate depot head.

7. The tasks and the mission's nature may not be disclosed. The strictest secrecy should be applied. The mission is declared, if necessary, as a reconnaissance, ordered for the protection of neutrality. The mission should be executed with the utmost urgency.

Stockholm, April 27, 1945.
By order,
A. Ljungdahl.
Chief of Air Staff.

The next day, April 28, Ljungdahl issued a new order to Beckhammar, this time regarding photography of Bornholm's coastline Sandvig - Svaneke - Nexö. However, Jutland was not included in "Save Denmark" (RD) – it was only Zealand (RDS) and Bornholm (RDB) that mattered.

It is unclear how much the four Danish pilots at F6 Karlsborg knew about the details of RD, RDS and RDB. But they were most likely aware that forming a union of the three Danish Brigade Air Unit groups, in Karlsborg, Kalmar and Östersund, was imminent. The F6 group in Karlsborg, therefore, decided to develop plans for attacks on selected locations in Jutland, which could then be presented to the combined Air Unit, when the union was formed. This was part of the ongoing training with the B17 aircraft. According to his statement, E. Møller was commissioned to design a plan for an attack on the German coastal fortifications in Hanstholm on Jutland's northwestern North Sea coast. Carlo was commissioned to create a plan for an attack on Aalborg Airport. It was logical that Carlo should take on Aalborg Airport, considering that he knew the airport as well as his own pocket. Carlo had been the leading person at a flying school there in the first year of the airport's existence, in 1938/39. During two years of the German occupation, in 1942 - 1944, Aalborg Airport was his workplace. No one knew that airport better than him. Below is Carlo's plan described for an attack on Aalborg Airport, translated into English. The Danish handwritten original version is preserved in the War Archives in Stockholm – the "Secrecy" classification was lifted as recently as on October 25, 2011. A copy of the plan is photographically reproduced in the Appendix.

Deliberations and Decisions.

The attack could be carried out with little or no loss, as there is no defence by enemy fighters, and it is likely that the anti-aircraft artillery is currently significantly reduced, as it is transferred to the Eastern and Western Front. The attack could therefore be carried out as a day-time operation, but since one can probably achieve a greater surprise early in the morning, this time should be preferable.

The target's location near the sea (10 minutes of flight time along the selected flight track) increases the moment of surprise and makes it possible to attack before the enemy can take any countermeasures.

The primary purpose of the attack should be to destroy the 30 He 111 [aircraft] and maintenance workshops. Since it is impossible to know in advance in which hangars the aircraft are parked, and the division is unable to destroy all the hangars, the target distribution can only be partially assigned before takeoff. The Division Commander must therefore, on arrival at the target, take the risk of making a low-pass over the open hangars to ascertain where the aircraft are stored, and then assign the targets over the radio.

Approach at the highest altitude would be preferable. The western heading, 20 km south of Aalborg, and continued flight on the same heading across the railway and the highway, south of the city, may mislead the enemy to believe that the attack is aimed at another target. Thereafter, by heading North and diving, the target can be reached in three minutes.

The return flight to the East can be done at minimum altitude over the hilly terrain north of the Limfjord (4/10 cloud cover does not provide sufficient protection.)

Since the enemy aircraft are inside hangars, 50-kg bombs will be handy. If there are aircraft outside of the hangars, they can be attacked with machine guns.

Due to a large number of hangars and their locations, it may be necessary for some aircraft to attack with a 45-degree pitch angle dive, to obtain a sufficiently broad coverage. If the air defence is very weak, one can let the planes drop the bombs one by one.

F6 Air Base, 2 Division   Map: 1: 300,000
Karlsborg   1: 100,000 Leaf No. over Denmark

Division Order No. 1
Situation: English and American forces have broken through the Western front, advanced up through Southern

141

Jutland and are now fighting on the line Esbjerg - Kolding.

The *Division* will attack Airport West near Aalborg. *Secondary target:* Airport East near Aalborg.

1. *Attack objects:* 30 He 111 in hangars, and workshops.

2. *Start:* 01.55 a.m. In groups.

3. *Formation:* Above the airbase. Elevation: 500 m.

4. *Approach:* Karlsborg - Varberg - Lille Vildmose - Point 10 km West of Støvring - Airport West.

5. The *attack:*

Approach: From the South. Heading North.

Target distribution: Aircraft A, B, C and D attack hangars and workshops 1, 2, 3 and 4. Aircraft E, F, G, H and I await orders by radio at an altitude of 2,000 meters, 5 km South of the cement factory Norden; leader of this group Lieutenant O.

Attack mode: A, B, C and D: 60-degree pitch angle dive. Other aircraft: according to order by radio.

Bomb drops: Series. Bombing distance: 20 m. One flight over targets.

6. *Return flight:* Hvorup - the coast between Asaa and Hals - Varberg - Gothenburg (Säve).

7. *Bomb and fuel requirement:* Load options 4.

8. *Identification:* Identification signal Alternative 1. Identification call Alternative 3.

9. Weather report: 01.00 a.m.

10. Communication: Division frequency No. 2. Radio silence until the target is reached.

11. After the mission: Refuelling and mounting of bombs. Load alternative 4. Contingency I. Further attacks depart from Säve.

12. I am in aircraft A.   *C. H. Sandqvist*
                                Division Commander.

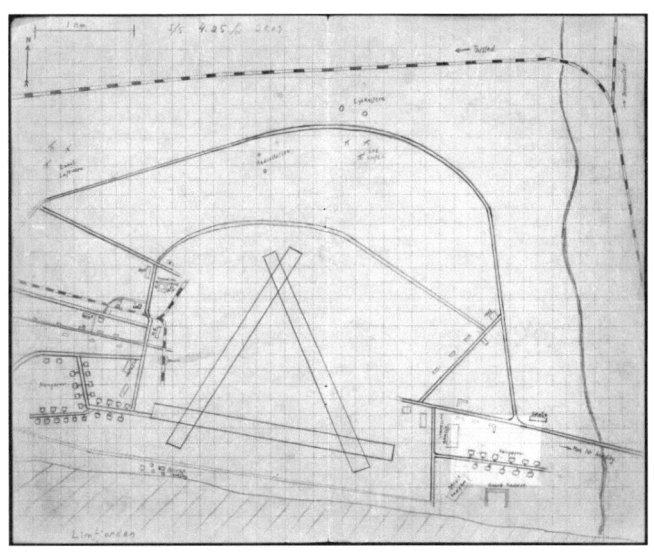

Sketch of Aalborg Airport, which was part of Carlo's plan

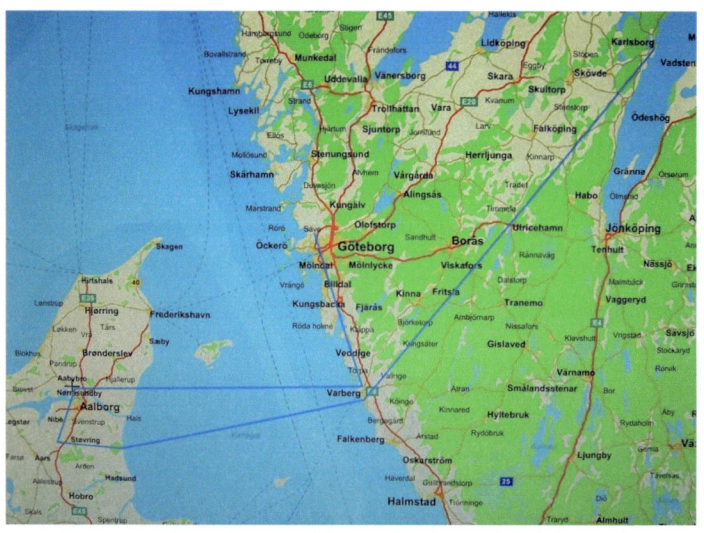

Map showing the route of the planned attack on
Aalborg Airport

A sketch of Aalborg Airport was included in the attack plan, developed at F6 in Karlsborg during the second half of April. The date of the attack was set for May 5, 1945! This date has etched itself into Denmark's history, however, not because of Carlo's attack plan. It is the date when Denmark celebrated its liberation after more than five years of the German occupation. The further development of the war would now catch up with the plans.

But before that happened, orders came from above. The three groups in the Brigade's Air Unit, which were divided into F4 Östersund, F6 Karlsborg and F12 Kalmar, should unite at F7 Såtenäs on 4 May. At F7, Carlo should present his attack plan to the entire Danish Brigade's Air Unit. Lieutenant Captain V. Holm (F12) recollects his surprise about the existence of the plan. It was not known to anyone outside of Karlsborg: "The

144

'Secret' label had worked!" He also raises the question of the identity of the "Lieutenant O", mentioned in the plan: "We had no Lieutenant O. So I assume that it was a group of Swedish volunteers who had signed up for operational training". It could have been the case, because Sweden had for a long time allowed the concept of *voluntary* Swedes participating in aid to Denmark. The "Save Denmark" plan included 300 aircraft from the Swedish Air Force. Therefore, some aircraft could be available for a Jutland operation as well.

Carlo's plan points out that one of its goals was to neutralize the about thirty Heinkel He 111:s, supposedly parked at Aalborg Airport. Carlo's knowledge of Aalborg Airport was a year old, and therefore possibly obsolete. But the Danish intelligence sources were very active and current information may have been available at F6 Karlsborg. The He 111 was a German twin-engine medium-sized bomber, that was indispensable in the first half of the war, and it was still being produced near the end of the war. The He 111 could also be used to carry remotely controlled rocket-propelled bombs of the Henschel Hs 293 type. Tests had been carried out with these bombs, on the He 177 bombers at Aalborg Airport, before April, 1945. Bomb storage and maintenance shops were also located at Aalborg Airport, which may have been the reason for the plan to include four workshops as bomb targets. The Hs 293 bombs were primarily intended for naval targets and were therefore a threat to the Danish Brigade's transfer to Denmark. To eliminate a division of the He 111 aircraft, capable of carrying Hs 293 bombs, would therefore be desirable. But were there any He 111:s at Aalborg Airport when the plan was to be carried out? The German Luftwaffe Kampfgeschwader II./KG 100 was based at Aalborg Airport from March, 1944, to February, 1945.

Emblem for Luftwaffe
Combat Squadron II./KG 100

Data from the Luftwaffe on January 10, 1945, show that, at that time, the II./KG 100 consisted of 32 operational He 177 bombers (out of a total number of 44). Could it be these 32 He 177:s that were in Carlo's mind? However, there was a significant shortage of fuel in the Luftwaffe, and most of the aircraft were on the ground and could not take off. It is interesting to note that ten days after the end of the war, on May 15, 1945, there were 201 German aircraft at Aalborg Airport, of which 47 were Me 109 fighters. As a result of the steadily declining occupied land and the imminent fall of the German Empire, many of Luftwaffe's units were relocated to Denmark during the last days of the war. However, there were neither He 111:s nor He 177:s Aalborg Airport on that day.

The takeoff from Karlsborg was set for 01.55 hours on May 5. If the nine B17 planes were B17C:s (which were offered to the Danish Brigade), Carlo set an altitude limit of 9,500 m on the legs: Karlsborg - Varberg - Lille Vildmose - Point 10 km West of Støvring. The total distance was 370 km, about one hour of flight with a cruise speed of 390 km/h, in zero-wind conditions. The arrival at the scene should be at dawn, so the speed should be adjusted according to that. The descent from "Point 10 km west of Støvring" North towards Aalborg Airport should be completed in three minutes at a maximum speed of 433 km/h.

The route across the Kattegat was carefully chosen to lie between the two German-occupied Danish islands, Læsø and Anholt. On Anholt there was a very advanced radar system with 1 Wasserman, 2 Wurzburg and 1 Freya antennas. There were also 2 Y-lines with marine radar. After the war, five of the Norwegian 7.5 meter Wurzburg-Riese antennas were converted to telescopes for radio astronomy after the war and placed at Onsala Space Observatory, South of Gothenburg; one of those telescopes is still there:

A German 7.5 meter Wurzburg-Riese radar antenna from World War II, now a radio telescope placed at Onsala Space Observatory, South of Gothenburg

Carlo had worked at the Air Notification Service of the State Civil Aviation Authority's Command Center on Aalborg Airport, which collected information about flights from the many German observation posts around Denmark. Therefore,

147

he knew very well the capacity of these radar facilities. There was no doubt that the facility on Anholt would detect the nine B17:s on a track from Sweden. So, it was necessary to make the Germans believe that this force was heading for a destination other than Aalborg.

During most of the war, Aalborg Airport had a solid air defence, which could defend this strategically important airport. The British Royal Air Force had discovered this during several raids, in which they also lost several aircraft. At its most advanced level, in 1944, the air defence consisted of four "Leichter Flakzug" (batteries of light anti-aircraft machine guns with a calibre of up to 36 mm) and two "Schwere Flakbatterie" (heavy cannons with a calibre from 60 to 159 mm), located adjacent to the airport. Leichter Flakzug was effective against flights below a height of 1,000 meters. Schwere Flakbatteri could fire heavy grenades up to a great height, where they would explode in aircraft formations at a predetermined altitude. Some of these air defence units were dismantled at the beginning of 1945 and transferred to the Eastern and Western fronts. Most of the units may have been completely removed from Aalborg Airport near the end of the war, as assumed in Carlo's plan, based on information probably obtained from reports from the Danish intelligence service.

Carlo's attack plan was never put to the test because the war would end first. Secrecy about the project was strict, probably also on a private level. It is unlikely that Carlo discussed it with Elsa at the dinner table in Karlsborg. She would probably have had problems to accept that her husband was planning a bombing attack with nine B17 aircraft against Aalborg Airport – only 10 km from their two children, Aage with his Grandma and Grandpa in Gug, and Gøsta with Knud and Helga in Aalborg. However, it was probably also not easy for Carlo. But anyhow, a short and pleasant time awaited. When it became known at the F6 airbase that the Danish pilots and technicians were about to leave Karlsborg and join the other Danish groups, from F4 Östersund and F12 Kalmar, at F7 Såtenäs, the staff at F6 staged a big farewell party for the Danes on April 28, 1945 – a party that would not be forgotten.

Menu for the F6 farewell dinner, held for the Danes
(depicting two B17:s)

Chapter 15: The Danish Brigade's Air Unit, Unified at F7 Såtenäs, May 4 - 5, 1945

Friday, May 4, 1945, early in the morning – a warm farewell to Elsa in the apartment in Karlsborg. Once again, the future was uncertain for Carlo. It was time for the small Danish Air Group at F6 to leave Karlsborg and move to F7 Såtenäs, which lay on the shores of Lake Vänern. It would unite there with the two other Danish air groups from Kalmar and Östersund. The train took them to Grästorp. They went on from there to the F7 airbase in Såtenäs, where they arrived in the morning. That it was at F7 Såtenäs that the entire Air Unit would be integrated, was partly because Såtenäs was at a suitable distance from the Sound, where the Danish Brigade's operations were expected to take place. It was also because there were a number of B17C:s at F7, which would eventually be made available to the Danish Air Unit.

The manor which became an officers' club at the
F7 Såtenäs airbase in 1940 (Photos 1940-1945: F7 Museum)

The Karlsborg group installed itself in a few barracks and then ate a hearty lunch in the stately officers' club, which was housed in a manor dating from 1392. During the fourteenth century, a few farms in the area were merged into one estate. Danes were already active on this Såtenäs property at that time:

Jöns Lage Posse, who came from Denmark, was the ancestor of the Posse family, which owned the estate for one and a half centuries, until about 1600. After that, various families lived on Såtenäs until 1938, when the Swedish State bought the estate. In 1940, the Swedish Air Force established an airbase at F7 Såtenäs. The current main building had its beginning as early as the end of the eighteenth century, while a major renovation took place in 1915. The most recent restoration occurred in 1998.

After lunch, the Danes went over to a large hangar to get acquainted with the B17C:s, which they would take over. The Kalmar group had also arrived, but the Östersund group would not arrive until the next day. Before the Danes reached the hangar, a minor drama took place. An English war-damaged twin-engine Mosquito bomber, escorted by two Swedish fighters, came in for a landing. The Mosquito landed at a high speed and hit the ground much too hard. The landing gear collapsed. The propellers broke loose and flew high into the air, while the rest of the plane slid straight towards the hangar at full speed. However, the hull managed to stop before reaching the concrete slab in front of the hangar. After a moment of intense activity at the airbase, the Danish inspection of the B17C:s could take place without further interruptions. Later in the afternoon, the Danes gathered in a room to plan for the coming 11-day period. At this meeting, Carlo gave an oral presentation of his plan for a combined B17 attack on Aalborg Airport.

The Swedish decision to gather the entire Danish Brigade Air Unit into a coherent unit at F7 Såtenäs, for an 11-day course, had been made at the turn of the months April/May. This was a couple of weeks after the final establishment of the overall operational plan to transfer the Brigade to Denmark.

Now it was time to prepare the Air Unit as well. On May 1, 1945, the head of the Danish Brigade's "Command for Military Refugees", Major General K. Knudtzon, sent a dispatch to the Swedish Armed Forces' Command Office, requesting that "15 aircraft be made available to the Danish Command, together with necessary ground equipment, etc.". On May 2 and 3, the request went to the Swedish Commander-in-Chief (ÖB), who forwarded it to the Chief of the Air Force, B. G. Nordenskiöld. Thereafter, the request was processed by the Air Staff. On May 5, the written response came back to ÖB from Nordenskiöld:

SECRET   *HEADQUARTERS*
                                                      AIR FORCE
                                                      No. H116

To the Commander-in-Chief.

Due to the request for an opinion about the petition received from the Command for Military Refugees on May 1, 1945, (Headquarters: Air Staff Communication No. H 59:13), I herewith respectfully report that the following main consequences will arise for the Air Force's war organization, if 15 B17C aircraft, together with certain other equipment, are made available to the Danish police troops.

1. It is proposed that the aircraft etc. in question are now based at F 7 (9 aircraft) and F 12 (6 aircraft).

2. The remaining B17C aircraft, currently assigned to F 7, are transferred to F 12, whereby no change needs to take place in the war organization of the latter airbase. For F 12, how-

ever, a certain additional cost arises, since some increased inspection work becomes necessary in the central workshops.

3. All B17A :s (currently 128) are divided equally between F4, F 6, and F 7. After the necessary service reserve has been deducted, a minor reduction in the war organization of these airbases becomes necessary; each of these should therefore – as far as the aircraft allocation is concerned – consist of a staff group of two aircraft and three divisions of 10 - 11 aircraft.

4. According to information obtained in advance from the Danish Command, some reinforcement with voluntary Swedish ground personnel will also be necessary for the Danish Air Unit to be operational. This personnel can be discharged without significantly affecting the war organization of the Air Force.

Since the above-mentioned consequences do not lead to any appreciable weakening of the war organization of the Air Force, I recommend, without hesitation, that the aircraft in question, etc., be made available to the Danish police troops.

Stockholm, May 5, 1945
B.G. Nordenskiöld
Chief of the Air Force.
/.
A. Ljungdahl.

This document confirmed what was already taking place;

the information therein had been disseminated to the various bodies. Therefore, on May 4, most of the Danish Brigade's Air Unit was already at F7 Såtenäs, with the rest on its way from Östersund. Fifteen B17C:s were ready to be transferred to the Danes.

After the long Danish planning meeting, Carlo and a comrade decided to walk in the beautiful park, where the officers' club was located. The following year, Carlo recalled what happened next in a Danish newspaper article:

In the evening, I was out walking with a comrade – we were strolling in the park near the officers' club. When I returned, there was no one in the club, and I really could not understand that. We turned on the radio right away, and when we heard that patriotic music was being played, we understood that something must have happened – the whole atmosphere was such. We then set out to search for the other pilots. We found them in the home of the Lieutenant Colonel, who had invited us to dinner to celebrate the event. We felt overwhelming joy and relief that Denmark had been spared the horrors of war. We knew that if our country had been actively involved in the war, it would not have looked different from the other war-torn countries of Europe. We readied the aircraft and painted Danish colours on them during the night, because we reckoned that we would be returning home together with the Brigade ….

The "event", worth celebrating with the F7 airbase commander, Lieutenant Colonel Folke Ramström, was the dramatic message from Field Marshal Montgomery's headquarters in Northern Germany: "The German troops in Holland, Denmark and Northwest Germany have capitulated!" The actual message, which was broadcast on Swedish Radio at 8.25 p.m., was that the German troops *would* capitulate, and that the capitulation would take effect at 8.00 a.m., in the morning of the next day, Saturday, May 5, 1945. The long-awaited code from Copenhagen to the Swedish government, which would activate the Danish Brigade transfer to Denmark, finally came on Friday at 10.15 p.m.: "Hans is sick"!

Now, there would be no B17 air attack on Aalborg Airport, or other strategic targets in Jutland. Instead, the Danish Brigade's Air Unit would concentrate on aerial support for the transfer of DANFORCE from Helsingborg to Elsinore, which would be initiated at 8 a.m. on Saturday. All the Danes were suddenly in a great hurry, and there was not much sleep to be had that night. The promised B17C:s were to be converted to Danish aircraft. Buckets with red and white paint were obtained quickly, and nine B17C:s on F7 were converted from Swedish to Danish aircraft during the night:

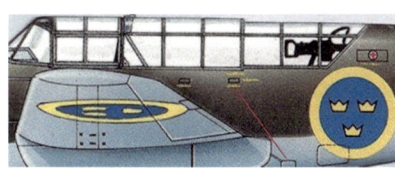 

The Swedish logo was painted over with the Danish logo, and an extra white outer ring to completely cover the Swedish

The outer white ring, painted around the red-white Danish logo did not really belong to the official Danish designation. It was added to cover the already existing yellow outer ring on the Swedish logo, which in its entirety was slightly larger than the Danish one. The two-tongued Danish naval flag was painted on the fins of the B17C:s. At least now, no one could be in doubt about to which nation these aircraft belonged. After a short night's sleep, the Danes got up at five o'clock on Saturday. Crews were now assigned to eight Danish B17C:s, and Carlo, as pilot, got Sergeant A. G. Johansen as his signaller. Then they all went through the plan for the day's activity.

The commander of the unified Danish Air Unit was Captain N. von Holstein-Rathlou. He had spent most of 1944 and 1945 at F11 Nyköping and had not trained on the B17 aircraft. His task was to obtain permission for the Air Unit to take off for Copenhagen with its eight B17:s. Lieutenant Captain Meincke, who was the oldest of the Danish B17 pilots, present at F6, would lead the group. The group was to fly southwards towards the Sound. As soon as it passed Halmstad, Meinke's signaller, Quartermaster H. K. Jensen, should contact the tower at Kastrup, Copenhagen's Airport, and request permission to land. At the same time, he should inquire about the current situation on the ground, regarding the Danish Brigade's progress with ships from Helsingborg to Elsinore, and further transport to Copenhagen. A steep dive over Copenhagen was not acceptable, but a minimum flight altitude should apply. On the way south over the Sound, the group should stay on the Swedish side, and be escorted by a division of Swedish fighters. Should it turn out that ground conditions on the Danish side of the Sound made it impossible to land at Kastrup, the group should head for Ljungbyhed in Sweden, land there and await new orders.

Now, it was primarily a matter of getting the aircraft ready for take-off. The newly painted B17C:s were towed out of the hangar and lined up on the tarmac in front of the large hangar. Nine B17C:s with Danish designations were now ready for inspection. These were the nine B17C:s at F7 which, according to the order of the Swedish Chief of the Air Force, would be transferred to the Danish Brigade. The remaining six B17C:s from F12 Kalmar, that also were included in the order, had not yet arrived in Såtenäs. The Danish pilots from Östersund had not arrived either: But now it was urgent to get the first squadron airborne, so that it could escort the Danish Brigade during its transfer to Denmark. The Östersund delegation could follow later, after it arrived in Såtenäs. Since the present Danish crew consisted of 8 pilots and 8 signallers (from F6 Karlsborg and F12 Kalmar), one of the nine Danish B17C:s, which had no crew yet, would remain parked at F7.

The Danish crew was ready. The engines on the B17C:s were warm. This was it. The only missing factor was permission to take off. Von Holstein-Rathlou tried to contact the head of the Danish Brigade, Major General Knudtzon, who should have arrived early in the morning with his staff in Helsingborg from Stockholm. However, due to technical problems, he could not make telephone contact with Knudtzon or anyone on his staff. He then tried to obtain a start permit from the Commander of the Swedish Air Force. This application went to the Swedish government via the Swedish ÖB and the Ministry of Defence. An answer finally arrived in the afternoon: the Swedish government gave its permission for the Danish B17 squadron to immediately take off for Copenhagen. However, the long-awaited permit came with one condition: approval was needed from the newly appointed government in Denmark, an approval that the Air Unit would be permitted to arrive in Copenhagen together with the main part of the Danish Brigade.

Here follows a picture sequence from the preparations for the departure of the Danish Brigade's Air Unit in Sweden, destined for Denmark, on Saturday, May 5, 1945 (all photos from

F7 Museum in Såtenäs):

Nine Danish B17C:s lined up outside the large hangar at F7 Såtenäs, ready for inspection

The Danish B17C crew at F7 is getting ready for departure to Denmark

*The Swedish F7 ground crew, which helped to prepare
the Danish B17C planes. From left: A. Bengtsson, F. Rösdahl,
G. Hammenfors, B. Appelgren, E. Wallin, N. Karlberg,
V. Bjärnsund, E. Strid, Ohlsson, and S. Strid*

*Swedish staff instructs the Danes about the B17C.
(In the background are a number of American B-24 "Liberator"
bombers, which have executed emergency landings)*

*Carlo inspects his
B17C. His signaller,
Sergeant A.G. Johansen,
stands behind him*

Warming of the engines on the Danish B17C:s has begun

The Danish crew in front of their B17C:s

The official portrait of the Danish B17C crew at F7 Såtenäs, May 5, 1945. Standing from left: Lieutenant Captain V. Holm, Lieutenant G. Bouet, Lieutenant A.G.K. Jessen, Lieutenant C.H. Sandqvist, Lieutenant Captain E.B. Meincke, Lieutenant D.K.W. Knudsen, Lieutenant Captain J.J. Ulrich, Lieutenant E. Møller, Sub-Quartermaster H.K. Jensen, Engineer C.H.E. Kallehauge, Private Øst Møller, Sergeant A.G. Johansen. Seated: Private B.L. Petersen, Sub-Quartermaster J.F. Rasmussen, Sergeant Hansen, Sergeant C. Møller

Chapter 16: The Return to Denmark

Såtenäs – Saturday, May 5, 1945, at 8.00 a.m.. Preparations for the Danish Brigade's Air Unit's flight to Denmark were in full swing. The engines on the Danish B17C:s were started for warming. At nine o'clock the engines were still running, but the planes were not moving. They remained stationary late in the morning, while the Danish commander, Captain von Holstein-Rathlou, tried energetically to get permission for the Air Unit to take off. Now, Karlsborg's group leader, Lieutenant Captain Meincke, decided that it was probably best to test-fly one of the planes, while waiting for the official take-off permission. Together with his signaller, Sub-Quartermaster Jensen, he took off with his B17C. Unfortunately, it soon started to go wrong. The engine started to cough, and threatened to quit already at 40 meters height,. The plane began to sink. Meincke throttled back and then rapidly up a couple of times – with no luck. He repeated this procedure a couple of times. Accompanied by some juicy Danish oaths, Meincke discussed the situation with Jensen over the radio. Jensen, a technician, had listened to the engine's trouble and suggested 1,800 rpm instead of full throttle. This solved the problem, and they could go in for an immediate landing. It was revealed that the spark plugs were sooted up due to the long idling. After thorough cleaning of all spark plugs on the B17C:s, they were again ready to take off for Denmark.

After lunch, it was decided to test-fly all B17C:s, and group flights were completed in 45 minutes. Carlo and Erik Møller were allowed to group fly for an hour and a quarter. After that, all aircraft were again on the ground, pending a take-off permit. The Swedish permission came surprisingly fast later in the afternoon and resulted in great joy among the Danish crew. Now it was up to von Holstein-Rathlou to fulfil the accompanying Swedish condition, that is, to obtain permission for take-off from the new Danish government.

Helsingborg – Saturday, May 5, 1945, at 8.00 a.m.. The Danish Brigade commander, Major General Knudtzon, had arrived in Helsingborg, where he installed his headquarters in Hotel Astoria around 7 a.m., after flying from Bromma to Ljungbyhed. The Danish Brigade's transfer from Helsingborg to Elsinore should have started at 8.00 a.m., which was the time for the German capitulation. However, it took another two hours before the first ship left the port of Helsingborg. The Danish navy had already sailed from Karlskrona to Malmö on the night between April 30 and May 1, to be close to Helsingborg. They were therefore ready to transport the Brigade soldiers across the Sound with all their military equipment. The naval flotilla consisted of about ten torpedo boats, minesweepers and cutters, that had managed to escape from the Germans during their "Safari" action in Denmark in August, 1943. This flotilla was subsequently moved to Helsingborg, where it arrived at six o'clock on May 5. The Danish icebreaker, "Mjølner", the ferries, "Stora Bœlt", "Holger Danske", "Dan" and "Svea", and other Danish ships – which had been in ports on Swedish west coast – would all take part in the transport of the Brigade soldiers. These soldiers had arrived in Helsingborg during the previous night. Swedish warships now escorted the Danes to the Swedish territorial border. Knudtzon and his staff left Helsingborg for the crossing to Elsinore with "Mjølner" in the middle of the day. It was a huge undertaking to transfer 4,759 men, women, and 3,500 tons of small calibre war equipment, from Sweden to Denmark. Large crowds of Swedes on the quays in Helsingborg waved goodbye to the Danish Brigade, and just as many Danes on the quays in Elsinore welcomed the Brigade back home to Denmark. The crossing of the Brigade from Helsingborg to Helsingør was not completed until the next day, May 6. After that, the transport of the troops to Copenhagen was carried out with trains, motor vehicles and bicycles. Although most things went smoothly, there was one intermezzo where a gunfire with some Danish Nazis led to three killed and fourteen wounded Brigade soldiers. Five of the attackers were killed and four were taken prisoner. But the German army was nowhere to be seen – it had capitulated. In Copenhagen, the Danish Brigade held a homecoming parade past madly cheering crowds.

The Danish Brigade marches into Copenhagen
on Sunday, May 6, 1945 (Photo: Mønthuset, Denmark)

Sadly, the Danish Air Unit from F7 Såtenäs did not arrive in time to participate in this joyous homecoming celebration; it was still awaiting the new Danish government's permission for takeoff.

To commemorate the formation of the Danish Brigade in Sweden on November 15, 1943, Mønthuset Danmark issued a gold-plated 75th anniversary medal in the autumn of 2018. The medal, which was free to residents of Denmark, shows the Brigade's landing in Elsinore on May 5, 1945:

75th anniversary medal (Photo: Mønthuset Danmark)

Meanwhile, time stood still in Såtenäs. The Danish B17 crew was anxious and impatient. Why did it take so long? When would the start permit come? Von Holstein-Rathlou had still not received an answer from Copenhagen by the late afternoon of May 5. Finally, he succeeded in getting in touch with the Prime Minister's Office in Copenhagen through a Danish diplomat's envoy. The Prime Minister's answer was hard to take: The Ministry considered that the matter was of insufficient importance at the present time to warrant an immediate decision. Instead came the order: WAIT! – "Wait for what?" was Carlo's first reaction. He, and the seven other Danish pilots now at F7, had been preparing for this day for a very long time. They had got access to the best aircraft that Sweden could offer and knew how to handle them in combat. If a battle action had arisen during the last days of the war, the Danish B17 squadron would have been the only real heavyweight part in the Danish Brigade. And now they were not permitted to come to "the King's City" [Copenhagen] on the day of triumph. It was a sad and disappointed group of Danish pilots and technicians, who finally tried to get some lost sleep at the end of this long day.

On the next day, May 6, the Östersund group also arrived at F7 Såtenäs, and the Danish Brigade's Air Unit became complete. This meant they could then *wait* as a complete Danish B17 squadron. Von Holstein-Rathlou gave the order to continue the training with the B17C:s. Without enthusiasm, but still hoping to of getting airborne towards Copenhagen, the Danes continued training in group flights. They also practised firing towards targets on the ground and in the air. Bombing exercises were not carried out, however. The local inhabitants around the F7 airbase noticed that there were planes in the air with Danish flags on the fins – this was unusual. And it was also unusual that some flight crews spoke "a strange form of Scanian" [the dialect of a southern Swedish province, close to Denmark]. But the war was over now, so the new situation at F7 was nothing for the locals to worry about.

The days passed by and the wait became long and difficult. Why did a start permit never arrive? The Danes at F7 became demoralized. Through radio and telephone contacts with relatives and friends in Denmark, they could feel the ecstatic joy that permeated Danish society after five long and difficult years of the German occupation. But they could not participate themselves. Carlo felt the longing for Aalborg severely now, since Elsa had left Karlsborg and gone back home. It was a consolation to know that his children had their mother back, but leaving F7 early would be the same as deserting for Carlo. That was not an option. There was still a hope that he could return shortly to Denmark with a Danish B17 squadron.

That hope was strengthened by the fact that Sweden now made a very generous offer to Denmark. The fifteen B17C:s, which the Chief of the Swedish Air Force had made available to the Danish Brigade at F7, could be purchased for the symbolic amount of two million Swedish kronor. The "offer" also included spare parts and engines, complete combat equipment, tools, weapons, ammunition, bombs, medical equipment, flight safety equipment such as a radio bearing range, and aviation fuel. Von Holstein-Rathlou immediately started preparations for transferring these aircraft and equipment to Denmark, and on May 12 everything was ready. However, early in the morning, came the next order from Copenhagen to the Air Unit: "COME HOME, IMMEDIATELY – BY TRAIN" – without aircraft and equipment!

It is impossible to describe the feelings of the Danish pilots and technicians, when they received this order. Seventeen hours later, at midnight between May 12 and 13, however, the entire Air Unit was back in Denmark, standing on Elsinore's quay. The feeling of disappointment and total humiliation lay heavy over this small remnant of the Danish Brigade, when it finally landed on Danish soil, without aircraft – a whole week after the arrival of the main part of the Brigade. There was no "Welcome Home" here! No one shouted "Hooray!". And two days later, Denmark rejected Sweden's generous offer of the 15 B17C:s aircraft, which were left at F7 Såtenäs.

In the Swedish National Archives in Stockholm, in National Defence Command Office's Secret Archive, the following is preserved: "F: documents concerning Danish (D) and Norwegian (N) police troops, etc., Vol. 1 (N) - 2 (D)". Document

D174 contains the Danish cancellation of the acquisition of the 15 B17C:s, which Sweden had offered Denmark for the generous, almost symbolic, sum of two million Swedish kronor. The cancellation was addressed to Major General P.H.T. Kellgren, Head of the National Defence Command Office, the Chancellery, Stockholm:

The Danish Brigade

Major General K. Knudtzon, Chief of
THE COMMAND OF MILITARY REFUGEES
Birger Jarlsgatan 14 - Tel 67 41 30 & 67 41 31
The equipment section
Fridhemsgatan 60 - tel 53 94 30 & 53 95 00

Confidential. Lb. No. 2178
Recommended. J. No. V. 4.

Stockholm, *May 14, 1945*

P. M.

regarding aircraft.

Major General K. Knudtzon has by Letter Lb. No. 21601, J.No. V 4 of May 1, 1945, made a request, that for the use of the Command, may be reserved

15 aircraft with necessary ground equipment etc.

Due to the events that have since occurred, a question was raised on May 5, 1945, as to whether the Command still maintained its desire to take over the above-mentioned 15 aircraft.

The case has since then been under consideration by the Danish General Command in Copenhagen, and an answer has now been received, according to which it may be honourably declared that the above request should be cancelled.

In the absence of the General: E. Lund, Captain.

This letter was transmitted via ÖB to the Chief of the Air Force, B.G. Nordenskiöld for an opinion. And thus the story of the Danish Brigade's Air Unit in Sweden 1944 - 1945 is finished! Why did the end become such a miserable affair? During the last two years of the war, seventeen Danish pilots had received training on both bombers and fighters in Sweden, as had Danish flight technicians and other ground personnel. They came originally from two separate air units in Denmark, the Army Air Troops and the Navy Air Entity. These two units, which had been merged in Sweden, now formed a potential seed for a budding united Danish Air Force. The 15 B17C:s could have become the aircraft, which Denmark needed to launch its own Air Force immediately after the war and thus retain its military pilots. But the General Command in Copenhagen believed that many of the German aircraft, which remained in Denmark after the war, could become part of a new Danish Air Force. British and American aircraft could be acquired after an initial transition period. Britain was an ally, that now took control of all the Danish airports, and Denmark felt that it was wiser to be associated with Britain rather than establish new contacts with Sweden. Unfortunately, this Danish approach would delay the establishment of a Danish Air Force until 1950. This also led to the loss of many Brigade pilots, who went into civil aviation.

Fifty years later, the Danish Brigade's Air Unit in Sweden 1944 - 1945 was honoured at a ceremony at F7 Såtenäs. Only a few elderly Danish Brigade pilots participated. A stand in the F7 Museum still draws attention to these fateful days, which took place at F7 Såtenäs on May 4 and 5, 1945.

The stand shows Colonel Vagn Holm, as he hands over the "Thank You" plaque from Denmark to Sweden on May 11, 1995, at the 50th anniversary ceremony, held at F7 Såtenäs. A list with the names of the Danish Brigade pilots and technical staff can be found on the right in the stand, and the text on the left reads:

Foreword by the author [V. Holm] *of this description of the Danish SAAB B-17 squadron in the Brigade.*

The mention of the Danish squadron in the Brigade is gradually fading into darkness. In Hirschsprung's book from 1945: "The Danish Brigade", there is a whole section about the squadron with 6 pages and 2 pictures.

In Gyldendal's: "Brigade" from 1993 there were 2½ pages and 2 pictures, and in the Danish Brigade Association's: "Refugee and soldier" from 1995 there were 2 lines and a small square of about 10 mm in an organization chart.

It is my hope that this report will help to preserve the memory of this unit, which was probably the most powerful of all the brigade's units. Only an operation against German forces in Denmark would have shown this to be true. Fortunately, such an action was not required. The squadron was disbanded after a "No, Thank You" from Denmark to purchase all aircraft and equipment for a symbolic price of 2 million kronor.

A "Yes, Thank You" for this purchase would have given Denmark an opportunity to create an Air Force, already in 1945, with the squadron's well-trained pilots and technicians, who came from the Army Air Troops and the Navy Air Entity.

Instead, the Air Force was first established in 1950, when many of our experienced pilots and technicians had already switched into civilian commercial aviation.

Vagn Holm

Exhibition stand in memory of
The Danish Brigade's Air Unit, at F7 Museum, Såtenäs

Chapter 17: Britain Surrenders Aalborg Airport to Denmark on January 1, 1946

On the front page of Sweden's largest morning newspaper, Dagens Nyheter, on Sunday, May 6, 1945, you can read about the events in Denmark on May 5, when the British liberated the country from the German occupation forces and took control:

COPENHAGEN, Saturday:

The British have conquered Denmark. Montgomery's paratroopers received a tumultuous reception when they travelled by car around Kongens Nytorv this afternoon. Only words, usually applied to southern festivals, are adequate to describe the atmosphere. Tanned boys were showered with flowers. Girls, women, and even old women climbed up on the trucks and accompanied the troops around the square.

Soldiers were pulled down from the trucks and carried in "golden chairs", accompanied by the cheers of the crowd. Hands reached out, handkerchiefs waved, cheers endured so long that they finally became hoarse whispers.

General Dewing, who represents the Allied Armed Forces and is expected to meet King Christian tomorrow, arrived in Copenhagen in a transport plane division. This was guarded by the fast-moving Spitfires which, just a few hours earlier, had left an airport near Hamburg, an airport that the airborne troops had conquered only a few weeks ago.

The Sixth Airborne Division is the general's entourage – boys who, on their merit list, include the landing in Normandy on D-Day …….

It did not take long before the British had full control of all airports in Denmark. One of their main targets was Aalborg Airport, the springboard to Norway, where the Germans had gathered many warplanes in the last days of the war in a vain attempt to protect them from the Allied forces. Now the Germans were forced to leave Denmark as soon as possible, but all their equipment was left behind under British supervision. Could this be an opportunity for the small Air Unit from the Danish Brigade, which had returned home from Sweden at midnight between May 12 and 13?

This Air Unit consisted of pilots and technicians from both the Army Air Troops and the Navy Air Entity. In Sweden, they had eventually combined as a functioning unit which, with the right planning, could have quickly formed a unified Danish Air Force after the war. But now they have instead separated again. The Army Air Troops, which included Carlo, settled at Lundtofte Airport just north of Copenhagen, while the Navy Air Entity returned to the Copenhagen Naval Air Station. Elsa was now at home in Aalborg, but Carlo continued in the Army Air Troops, now as volunteer with a three-month notification period. His salary was not large, 465 Danish Crowns per month. In principle, there was also a supplement on flight duty, but there were no aircraft to fly.

Carlo had still not had the opportunity to travel to Aalborg for a reunion with Elsa and the children. He lived in Copenhagen but spent the days at Lundtofte. In the evenings, he visited friends or his brother, Børge, who lived in Herlev, also north of Copenhagen. Børge had already returned to Denmark from Sweden on May 7, where he had spent a few weeks after the White Buses had rescued him from the German concentration camps in Buchenwald and Neuengammen. The joy of seeing Børge again was great. But Børge had very bad news to convey to Carlo: on April 4, just one month before the end of the war, their father had died of a heart attack at the age of only 62 years. Carlo was struck by this news, which followed so soon after the severe disappointment of the Air Unit's humiliating return to Denmark. He visited his father's grave with his mother on the following Sunday, and sought further comfort from his sister, Nina, during long walks in the nearby woods. The urgency to return to Aalborg was even greater now, and he applied for fourteen days of leave, starting on June 20.

Before Carlo went to Aalborg, he visited Rassow, a fellow prisoner from the Horserød concentration camp. Rassow told him that Wassermann – the German Hauptwachtmeister in the Horserød and Frøslev concentration camps, with whom Carlo had been on friendly terms – had returned to Germany. Wassermann was glad that Carlo had managed to escape from the train, but he was worried that Carlo would be captured again. He was proud that it was one of his prisoners, who had deceived the German prison guard, "Hundertfünfzig-meter-zurück", a person whom Wassermann also despised. When Wassermann found out that Carlo and Elsa had managed to get to Sweden, he had said that it was good!

On Wednesday, June 20, 1945, a train from the south drove slowly into Aalborg Central Station, where it stopped. Eight months and ten days had passed since another train, with Carlo on board, had made the same journey – with Carlo as a German concentration camp prisoner and hostage. Now he came as a free Danish aviation officer. An emotional reunion would take place again. Carlo quickly stepped down onto the platform and searched for a familiar face among the many passengers who swarmed around the train. Finally he saw them in the distance – Elsa with Gøsta on her arm, Aage between her and his Grandma and Grandpa, and on the other side, Knud and Helga, Gøsta's "parents" for the past nine months: "Welcome home, Carlo!"

The leave passed quickly, of course, and soon it was time for Carlo to return to Copenhagen. But on June 30, a telegram suddenly arrived to Lieutenant C. H. Sandqvist from his commander, Lieutenant Colonel L. Bjarkov: "Register as an interpreter at Squadron 2 Aalborg, on July 2, 1945". Now, Carlo would remain with his family in Aalborg. He would be back on Aalborg Airport after a fourteen month absence – now, however, under completely different conditions.

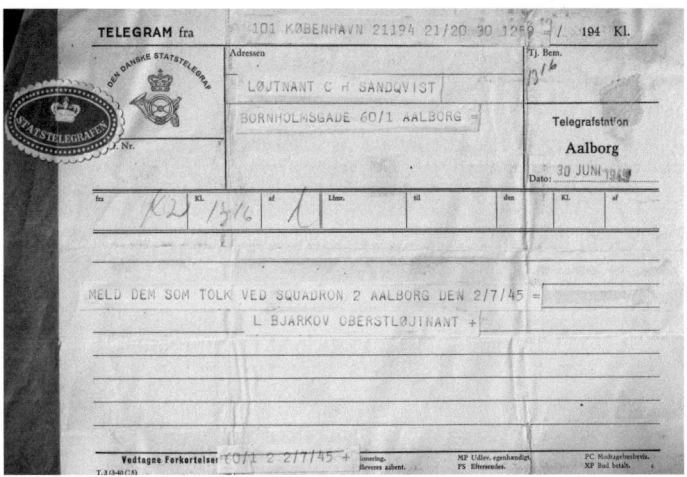

Lieutenant Colonel Bjarkov's telegram to Carlo

Aalborg Airport had now been abandoned by thousands of Germans, who were in a hurry to wander south after the capitulation. The new host was the Royal Air Force (RAF) 2 Squadron, 8403 Wing, whose commander was Squadron Leader Nichols. However, some German pilots and technicians remained to help with the huge German aircraft collection that remained on Aalborg Airport. Carlo spoke fluent English and German, which was important for his job as an interpreter. But he was quickly promoted to liaison officer between the British and the Danes, and there was much to deal with. As early as May 15, there were 201 German aircraft at Aalborg Airport. They included 47 Messerschmitt Bf 109 and 67 Focke-Wulf Fw 190 – both types were fast fighter planes – and 39 Arado Ar 96 training aircraft. These were aircraft which the Germans had transferred to Aalborg in the final stages of the war to protect them against the advancing Allied and Russian troops in Germany. A few months after the end of the war, the number had increased to just over 400 aircraft. They included single-engine Stukas bombers, twin-engine Heinkel He 111 and Junkers Ju 88 bombers, twin-engine Messerschmitt Bf 110 attack aircraft, and more. The British were in full swing, gathering all German aircraft in Northern Jutland at Aalborg Airport. For this purpose, they had to keep some German pilots and technicians in North Jutland.

This German air armada implied a great wealth, worth many millions of Danish Crowns. Carlo desired two of these aircraft for training Danish private pilots in Aalborg. The Army Air Troops wanted some of the Bf 109:s to establish a Danish Air Force and thus recruit the Danish pilots who remained in service, and even increase the number. The British, however, had other plans. A selection of aircraft should be flown south towards Schleswig and from there across the English Channel to the British Isles. But most of the German planes should be blown up! The rationale for this massive destruction of precious aircraft was to ensure that Germany would not have the opportunity to re-establish itself as an Air Power in the future.

However, the more than 600 buildings at Aalborg Airport – barracks, hangars and bunkers – remained unscathed. During the autumn of 1945, an unparalleled blasting activity took place, and large aircraft junkyards were established at several locations at the airport.

Royal Air Force (RAF) 2 Squadron, 8403 Wing company, in front of the German administration building at Aalborg Airport, late autumn, 1945. The Danish liaison officer, Lieutenant C. H. Sandqvist, sits in the second row, number two from the left

After this destruction campaign, the British began preparations to hand over Aalborg Airport to the Danish authorities. At the beginning of December 1945, the new Danish head of Jutland and Funen airports, Lieutenant Colonel T. A. Poulsen, inspected Aalborg Airport (which also included the two smaller airports, Aalborg East and Aalborg Sea). He announced:

"For the time being, we will take over the surveillance and administration of the airports after the Brirish. Lieutenant C. H. Sandqvist, who has shown himself to be an excellent man, will become commander of the airports, and as such will be responsible for the actual management of the airports."

Both military and civil aviation would operate on Aalborg Airport in the future. When asked how many aircraft the Army

Air Troops had at its disposal in December, 1945, Poulsen answered: "Two!" They were two British Proctor III single-engine three-seater training aircraft, that had just arrived at another airport in Jutland, but more would come. A small Danish Royal Air Force was initially the modest goal.

Now the transfer of Aalborg Airport from Britain to Denmark would soon take place. On December 8, RAF 8403 Wing held a farewell party in Aarhus City Hall. Royal Air Force Denmark had its headquarters in many buildings in Aarhus and Havreballegaard Woods outside of Aarhus. All those buildings would be vacated on the last day of the year. Additional farewell parties would take place on later occasions around Denmark.

Invitation to RAF farewell parties

During the latter part of December, most of the RAF 2 Squadron, 8403 Wing company travelled from Aalborg Airport south to South Schleswig in northern Germany. Only a few British officers remained to take part in the official handover ceremony, which was scheduled for New Year's Day, January 1,

1946.

Tuesday, January 1, 1946 – not since the German invasion of Denmark on April 9, 1940, had Aalborg Airport been under Danish sovereignty. More than five years of German ruling were followed by eight months of British ruling. It was finally time for Denmark to regain control of one of its most important airports. On behalf of the Royal Air Force, Squadron Leader Nichols now handed over Aalborg Airport to Lieutenant C. H. Sandqvist, who received it on behalf of Denmark and thus became the airport commander.

Below are some photos from the handover ceremony, which was held at the old German administration building:

The transfer of Aalborg Airport from Britain to Denmark: Squadron Leader Nichols in front of the last RAF officers at the airport, Flight Officer Curt and Flight Lieutenants Michell, Karton and Svopshire

In his speech to the Danes, Squadron Leader Nichols said, among other things: "*My men, who have already travelled to*

Germany, were really sad to leave your city, where they have spent a wonderful time. To show our gratitude and express our best wishes for the future, we want to hand over the airport to the Danish authorities on the first day of the new year. We express our thanks to the Danish army and the Park Command, and to all our friends in Aalborg. Thank you for all your kindness, help, and hospitality."

To replace the British company, there was now a Danish military division from the 3rd Regiment's 5 Squadron that would take over Aalborg Airport's surveillance under Carlo's command.

The transfer of Aalborg Airport from Britain to Denmark: Carlo in front of the Danish military division from the 3rd Regiment's 5 Squadron

In his speech of thanks to the British, Carlo said, among other things: *"This day, when we hoist Dannebrog* [Danish flag] *on our own pole at Aalborg Airport, we have been looking forward to for so many years. We know very well, that if Britain had given up in 1940, when it looked the darkest, Denmark would never have become a free nation again. As we thank the Royal Air Force for its efforts and what it has handed over to us today, we express the hope for a great future for Aalborg Airport. And we hope that you, from the other side of the North Sea, will come to visit us again. You will always be welcome. Thank you for what you have done!"*

Many guests were present at this ceremony. They represented, among others, the Danish Army Air Troops, the Danish Military, the Park Command, the Civil Aviation Authority, the Ministry of Labour, the Police Authority in Nørre Sundby, the County Council, the Refugee Administration, etc. – and Elsa, as the wife of the incoming commander.

Carlo and Squadron Leader Nichols in front of the invited guests: In the foreground among the guests, Ritmester A. Møller, Captain Christiansen, County Councilor Scheving and Engineer Ørum. Elsa is visible in back (at Carlo's shoulders)

The transfer of Aalborg Airport from Britain to Denmark:
Left: Squadron Leader Nichols and Carlo. Right: Squadron
Leader Nichols lowers a rather windtorn RAF flag

The transfer of Aalborg Airport from Britain to Denmark:
Carlo hoists Dannebrog, and Aalborg Airport is Danish again,
for the first time in almost five years and nine months

Raising Dannebrog over Aalborg Airport filled Carlo with almost ecstatic joy and pride. From the beginning, he had been involved with this airport; run an a flying school before the war, seen how the Germans expanded the airport and used it for their daily and nightly patrols of the North Sea, and for their transports to their bases in Norway. He had spied on the Germans' activities at the airport and reported back to England. It was also here that the Germans captured him and put him in a concentration camp. Furthermore, it was this airport Carlo had planned to bomb with the advanced Swedish B17 dive bombers. Now he was the Commander of Aalborg Airport, with all the responsibilities and opportunities, that opened for him. It was truly a day of joy.

Epilogue: Aalborg Airport, 1946 - 1951, Aage's Perspective

What happened after that? In this epilogue, I shall summarize these events. When Carlo became the Commander of Aalborg Airport, the childhood of his sons was indeed affected.

The first week in 1946 was moving time for Carlo and Elsa, Aage and Gøsta. They left the apartment on Bornholmsgade in Aalborg and moved out to the Commander's residence at Aalborg Airport. Aage had started first grade in the "Minoria" school in Aalborg and now had seven kilometres to the school. It was no longer possible to walk to school, so a car transport was needed. There were not many cars in Aalborg at that time, but Carlo had access to a German Ford Eifel. Now it was up to Elsa to get a driver's licence as quickly as possible. This meant private tuition on the German-built runways with Carlo as a driving instructor. There were no playmates at the airport. However, there were many exciting "playgrounds", long laby-rinth-shaped trenches, concrete bunkers with strange round meter-high "towers", and an endless number of hangars. But the best part was when Carlo took Aage to one of the aeroplane junkyards and let him sit in the cockpit of a demolished Messerschmitt Bf 109.

It may seem irresponsible to let a seven-year-old run around in trenches and play in German bunkers. But a major clean-up campaign had already taken place at the airport, and the nearest areas were checked by Carlo, himself. The most dangerous moment, however, came from the Danish side. One day, Carlo and Aage had taken a trip around the airport by car. They parked the car at a hangar and walked out onto the nearby field. Suddenly, several shots were heard up close. Carlo threw himself on top of Aage and they fell to the ground. They had to crawl through the tall grass back to the hangar. Carlo got Aage into the car and quickly set off towards a couple of Danish soldiers with rifles, who were strolling across the field. They had had been hunting hares and inadvertently sent the bullets in the direction of the Commander and his son. The soldiers were transported immediately to the military detention centre.

One of several aircraft junkyards at Aalborg Airport, filled with demolished German warplanes. In the background some of the many hangars are seen. (Photo: Jens Langeland-Knudsen)

The future of Aalborg Airport would include both military and civilian air traffic. During 1946, negotiations were conducted at the government level on how Aalborg Airport would handle these two tasks. From the beginning, Carlo had focused his visions on the civilian part. He had already in the summer of 1945 applied for a concession to conduct a flying school, sightseeing, taxi and postal flights, as well as aerial photography. As early as March 6, 1946, the approval came, and Carlo began to procure aircraft for these activities. On July 29, he landed his first aircraft, a three-seater Auster, picked up in Copenhagen. Shortly afterwards, he bought a two-seater KZ III, which was equipped for training. On October 11, 1946, one-third of Aalborg Airport was transferred back to the civilian authority, Statens Lufthavnsvœsen, while the remainder went partly to the Ministry of War and partly back to private owners from before the war. Carlo would henceforth concentrate on his civilian aviation operations, while at the same time becoming a Captain in the reserve of the Army Air Troops. The old German administration building was renovated and converted into a passenger terminal and an administration building. Carlo and his family were allowed to stay in the Commander's residence until the beginning of 1947. After that, they moved to the nearby old German Officers' Mess, which had been partially renovated.

In the autumn of 1947, Aage had learned how to ride a bike and now, as an eight-year-old, he was considered old enough to cycle the 7 km long distance to the school in Aalborg. This was quite safe since there was hardly any road traffic at that time. However, he would have to cross the runways at the airport. He was reminded by his mother: "When you get to the runways, you must first look to the left, and then to the right, and if no DC-3 is coming, you may cross the runways". On the way home, there was often a strong headwind at the airport's open area. But the compelling sight of his father's two planes, and perhaps some DC-3, in front of the administration building, gave him the strength to fight the headwind.

Aalborg Airport 1947. A Danish and a Norwegian DC-3
commercial aircraft in front of the administration building.
Carlo's Auster and KZ III can be seen near the building
(Photo: Aalborg Airport)

When Aage came home to the officers' mess, it was often
the trenches and bunkers that entertained him before it was time
for homework. There were no playmates, but actually lots of
children, German children, behind barbed wire fences, just
across the road from the officers' mess. They were German
refugees. At Aalborg Airport, three areas were filled to the brim
with German refugees, 18,000 in total. The refugees were not
allowed to leave the camps, which Danish soldiers strictly
guarded. Many of the refugees were children, but Aage was not
allowed to play with them. In the beginning, Aage and the
German children often stood and just looked at each other
through the barbed wires. One time, a German child mustered
the courage to say to Aage: "Holz, bitte?" Aage had already
learned a lot of German, because Carlo had engaged two women and a man from the camp as domestic help to make life
more bearable for some of the refugees,. They were "Erika"
from Germany, "Erna" from Latvia, and "Gerhard" from Germany who was the chauffeur. All three spoke German with
Aage and Gøsta. Erna eventually became part of the family, but
Erika and Gerhard went home to Germany after a few years.
The German children were miserably cold and begged for fire-

wood. As a "secret" task, Aage used to break planks from a nearby abandoned barrack and give to the children on the other side of the fence. The German refugees remained at Aalborg Airport for several years, and the last ones did not return to Germany until 1949[4].

During the summer of 1947, Carlo contacted Lydia in Copenhagen, and they agreed to let the two brothers, Erik and Aage, regain some contact with each other for a few weeks. Aage went to Lydia in Copenhagen for a couple of weeks, and Erik came to Carlo at Aalborg Airport. Copenhagen's big city was a stimulating experience for Aage, and being back with his father at Aalborg Airport, like before the war, was just as exciting for Erik. There were many flights, where Carlo let both Erik and Aage take over control of the plane, although not until a safe altitude was reached.

Erik, Aage and Gøsta with one of Carlo's planes
at Aalborg Airport, in the summer of 1947

---

4 In total, there had been 238,000 German refugees in Denmark. The majority were women, children and elderly, who had fled to Denmark from the advancing Soviet front in the war's final stages. They thus accounted for 5% of Denmark's entire population and cost the Danish state 428 million Danish crowns.

Erik, Aage and Gøsta at home on the terrace of the old German Officers' Mess at Aalborg Airport, in the summer of 1947. In the background is Aage's favourite bunker

The development of Carlo's air business proceeded fast. Many pilots were trained at the flight school, sightseeing flying was popular, and aerial photography of farms all over Denmark was started. In 1948, the military took over the entire western part of Aalborg Airport. Carlo and his family had to leave the Officers' Mess and move again – to the eastern side of the airport, now into another German barrack that has also been renovated. It was located on the site of the current passenger terminal. Aage was happy with this move, because he no longer had to cycle across the runways and the airport's open terrain to get to school. On the other side of the road from the new residence, there was again a German refugee camp, but it would soon be emptied when the last Germans returned to their homeland. Carlo's own civilian aircraft fleet now consisted of one Auster, two KZ III:s, and two KZ VII:s which had room for four people, including the pilot.

Carlo's five planes in front of the administration building at Aalborg Airport, 1949

After some years, Carlo and Elsa's appetite for adventure took over again. They decided to sell the air business and emigrate to Canada with Aage, Gøsta and Erna in May, 1951. In Canada, Carlo established an aerial photography company, that a few years later covered all of eastern Canada and even expanded into New York State in the United States. Aage's Grandma and Grandpa also moved to Canada in 1953 to be close to children and grandchildren, and they acquired a farm in Ontario. However, they moved back to Denmark about ten years later. Knud and Helga and their daughter also emigrated to Canada but continued a few years later to the United States. In the mid-1960s, Carlo reduced his business' size to a family level, and with Elsa moved from Ottawa to a lakefront villa on Lake Ontario. It lay directly across the Bay of Quinte from Canada's largest military airbase, Royal Canadian Air Force

Base Trenton. Here they could sit on their lawn and enjoy the flight of aircraft over the base, only 3 km away on the other side of the bay. Their children were far away, but children and grandchildren came to visit regularly. Erik's ambition to become an airline pilot failed due to a motorcycle accident, but he later became a cabin chief at Sterling Airways. Aage met a Swedish girl at the University of Maryland and moved to Sweden with her in 1971. Eventually, Aage became a Professor of Astronomy at Stockholm University. Gøsta became active in the tourism industry in Manitoba. Carlo died in his home on February 11, 1985 (four years before Elsa), on the day before Aage arrived for a visit.

With that, I now conclude the story of the Danish Brigade's Air Unit and my father, Carlo Sandqvist's role in it.

Appendix

The Original Document of Carlo's Plan for the Attack on Aalborg Airport, 1945

The original document is preserved in the Swedish War Archives

List no: 640, Secret (H) and Qualified Secret (KH) documents (Secrecy status repealed on 2011-10-25)

Archive: Västgöta Air Flotilla

Department: The staff department with the flotilla expedition

Series title: Flotilla Staff Order (Neutrality Act)

Time: 1943 - 1944 (+1945)

Series: BII (includes also BIII 1945)

Volume no: 1

Overvejelser og Bestræbelser.

Angrebet skulde kunne gennemføres med ringe eller helt uden Tab, da der ikke findes fj. Jagerforsvar og man maa regne med at Lo. paa nuværende Tidspunkt af Krigen er stærkt reduceret, idet det er overført til Øst- og Vestfronten. Angrebet skulde altsaa af den Grund kunde udføres som Dagangreb, men da man vel nok maa regne med større Overraskelsesmoment tidligt paa Morgenen, maa dette Tidspunkt være at foretrække.

Maalet nære Beliggenhed ved Havet (10 Min. Flyvetid ad valgte Rute) forhøjer Overraskelsesmomentet, og gør det muligt at udføre Angrebet inden Fj. kan foretage Modforholdsregler.

Angrebet maa gaa ud paa først og fremmest at ødelægge de 30 stk. 111 samme Reparationsværkstederne og da det paa Forhaand er umuligt at vide i hvilke Hangarer Mask. staar kan Maaludelingen kun blive delvis inden Starten. Div.ch. maa ved Ankomsten til Maalet tage Risikoen ved en kort Overflyvning over de aabne Hangarer forst konstatere hvor Mask. befinder sig, og saa gennem Radioen anvise Maalene, og div. ikke er i Stand til at ødelægge alle Hangarerne.

194

Antgrning paa største Højde maa
vare at foretrække, idet den vestlige Flyve-
retning 20 km S/ Aalborg og Fortsat
over Jernbanen og Landevejen N.S. fra denne
By maaske kan faa Fj. til at tro at
Angrebet gælder andre Maal. Ved derefter
at svinge mod Nord og dykke vil Maalet
kunne naas paa 3 Min.

Fremrgrning paa laveste Højde kan i
det detynerede Terrain N.f. Limfjorden gennemføres mod Øst. (Fo Skydskke giver ikke Skjul nok)

Da de G. Mask. blinder sig i Hangaren
vil 50 kg Minebomber have god Virkning.
Skulde der staa Mask. paa fri Mark
kan disse beskydes med Maskingeværer.

Paa Grund af Hangarernes store Længd og Beliggen-
heden kan det blive nødvendig for at faa
tilstrækkelig stor Spredning, at lade nogle af
Maskinerne angribe i 45° Dykvinkel Er hv.
meget svagt kan man lade Mask. falde Bomber-
ne Bombevis.

6' Flotilje 2 Division   Kort: 1:300 000
Karlsborg, den 5/5 1945 Bil.   1:100 000 Blad Nr
                                        over Danmark.

Divisionsbefaling Nr 6
Mundtlig.

Situation: Engelske og amerikanske Styrker
er efter Gennembruk paa Vestfronten
gaaet op gennem Sønderjylland og kæm=
per nu i Linjen Esbjerg – Kolding.
Divisionen skal angribe Flyveplads West
        ved Aalborg. Sekundær Maal:
        Flyveplads Øst ved Aalborg.

1. Angrebsmaal er: 30 He 111 i Hangarer og
                   Værksteder.

2. Start: Kl: 01,55. Gruppevis.

3. Samling: Over Flyvepladsen. Højde:
                   500 m.

4. Anflyvning: Karlsborg – Varberg – Lt. Vild-
                   mose Pkt. 10 Km V. f.
                   Støvring – Flyveplads Øst.

196

5. _Angreb:_
   Indledning: Fra Syd. Hør N.
   Maalfordeling: Mask. A. B. C og D angr.
   Hangarer og Værksteder K. 2. 3 og
   4.

   Mask. 6. F. G. H. og J afventer
   Ordre pr Radio i 2000 m.s
   Højde 5 km S.f. Cementfa-
   briken Norden. Heder før
   Gr. Løjen. O.

   Angrebstype: A. B. C og D. 60° Styrtvinkel
   Øvrige Mask.: nærmere Ordre
   pr Radio.

   Bombeladning: Serie. Bombeafstand: 20 m
   1 Overflyvning.

6. _Tilbageflyvning:_ Hoorup — Kysten mell.
   Asaa og Hals. — Varberg-
   Göteborg. (Søre)

7. _Bombe og Brandskudstrustning:_
   Kastalternativ 4.

8. _Igenkending:_ Igenkendingssignal All. 1.
   faat ~ -- 3.
   Kontrolpunkt

9. Vejrrapport: Til 01.00.

10. Signaltjeneste: Div. frekvens Nr. 2. Radio otarshed til Maals er near.

11. Efter foretagendet: Tankning og Ophæng= ning af Bomber. Last= alternativ 4. Beded= skab I. Videre Angreb udgaar fra Sive.

12. Beger i Maskine Ch.

Øbilandqvist
Div. ch.

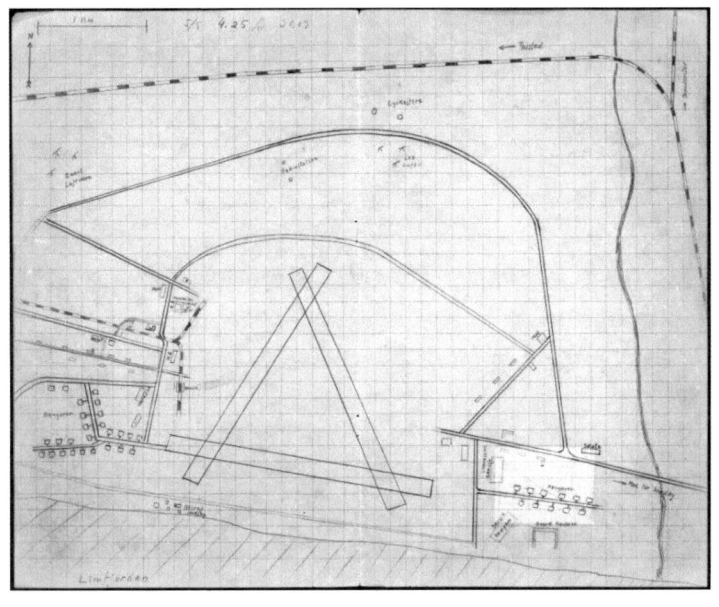

Sources

The Swedish War Archives in Stockholm

The Swedish National Archives Marieberg in Stockholm
Lantförsvarets kommandoexpedition, Secret Archive,
F: documents concerning the Danish and Norwegian police
troops etc. Vol. 2

N. von Holstein-Rathlou (1945): *BRIGADENS FLYVERSTYR-KER*, in "Den Danske Brigade" (editors N. Grunnet and B. Demer), Hirschsprungs Forlag, p. 197.

N.-A. Nilsson (1965): *DANSKA BRIGADENS FLYGSTYRKOR I SVERIGE*, in "Meddelande från SVENSK FLYGHISTORISK FÖRENING" Nr 12, Dec. 1965, p. 10.

U. Torell (1973): *Hjälp till Danmark. Militära och politiska förbindelser 1943-1945*. Almänna Förlaget.

Niels Helmø Larsen (1985): *DEN DANSKE BRIGADE. Den danske flyverstyrke og deres fly i Sverige under krigen*, Dansk Flyvehistorisk Forening. Særtryk 2/85.

H. Kofoed (1992): *Tyske fly i Danmark 15 maj 1945*. Flyveshistorisk Tidsskrift 4/92, p. 80.

V. Holm (1995): *Danska Brigadens flygstyrka 1944-1945*. Svensk Flyghistorisk Tidskrift 6/95, p. 6.

B. Widfeldt and Å. Hall (1997): *SAAB 17. Den första egna konstruktionen.* Air Historic Research.

A. C. Johansen (1999): *FLUGPLATZ AALBORG – WEST. DEN TYSKE UDBYGNING AF AALBORG FLYVEPLADS 1940 – 1945.* Eget forlag.

S. E. Bendix-Almgreen (1999): *SAAB 17 och Danmark. Speciellt historiens dunkle punkter.* Svensk Flyghistorisk Tidskrift 3/99, p. 17.

S. E. Bendix-Almgreen (2000): *SAAB B17 – Den Danske Brigades kampfly,* in "Danmarks Tekniske Museum Årbog 1998 -1999", p. 36.

H. Skov Kristensen, C. Kofoed and F. Weber (2012): *BOMBER OVER DANMARK. Vestallierade Luftangreb under 2. Verdenskrig.* Anden udgave. Nyt Nordisk Forlag Arnold Busck A/S.

The author in front of the three types of aircraft that played a decisive role in Lieutenant Sandqvist's pilot life: Tiger Moth, KZ III and Saab B17. The aircraft are located in the Technical Museum of Denmark in Elsinore. The Saab B17 plane, with the Danish nationality designations, is a gift from Sweden to Denmark, and was handed over in connection with the 25th anniversary, commemorating the Danish Brigade's Air Unit at F7 Såtenäs on 4 - 5 May 1945.